the sadat lectures

the sadat lectures
words and images on peace 1997–2008

Edited by Shibley Telhami

with contributions by

Jehan Sadat, Ezer Weizman, Jimmy Carter, Henry Kissinger, George Mitchell,
Nelson Mandela, Kofi Annan, Mary Robinson, James Baker,
Mohamed ElBaradei, Aaron David Miller

U.S. Institute of Peace Press
Washington, D.C.

United States Institute of Peace
1200 17th Street NW, Suite 200
Washington, DC 20036-3011
www.usip.org

First published 2010

Artwork courtesy of The Anwar Sadat Chair for Peace and Development, University of Maryland. Photographs by John Consoli. Cover art by Lelia Dunsmore (1960–2007).

Printed in the United States of America

The paper used in this publication meets the minimum requirements of American National Standards for Information Science—Permanence of Paper for Printed Library Materials, ANSI Z39.48-1984.

Library of Congress Cataloging-in-Publication Data

The Sadat lectures: words and images on peace, 1997–2008 / edited by Shibley Telhami; with contributions by Jehan Sedat ... [et al.]
    p. cm.
ISBN 978-1-60127-037-5 (pbk. : alk. paper)
1. Arab-Israeli conflict—1993—Peace. 2. Peace-building—Middle East. I. Telhami, Shibley. II. Sedat, Jehan. III. United States Institute of Peace.
 DS119.76.S22 2010
 956.05'4—dc22
                                                              2009039686

CONTENTS

FOREWORD
Jehan Sadat   vii

INTRODUCTION
A Decade of Perspectives on Peace, by Shibley Telhami   1

1. Ezer Weizman   16
2. Jimmy Carter   23
3. Henry Kissinger   34
4. George Mitchell   43
5. Nelson Mandela   59
6. Kofi Annan   66
7. Mary Robinson   71
8. James Baker III   79
9. Mohamed ElBaradei   86

CONCLUDING THOUGHTS
America and Arab-Israeli Peace, 1997–2009, by Aaron David Miller   95

CONTRIBUTORS   107

SADAT ART FOR PEACE   center insert

FOREWORD

JEHAN SADAT

The Sadat Lecture for Peace at the University of Maryland has provided a fitting tribute to the legacy of my late husband, President Anwar Sadat. Some of the lecturers were leaders I had known when I was first lady of Egypt. Jimmy Carter and Henry Kissinger were two men who had become close to President Sadat and who continued to be close family friends. Ezer Weizman, for whom President Sadat had much affection, never failed to call me on the date of Sadat's assassination every year until he passed away. But all lecturers were distinguished world leaders I personally admired, including those I met for the first time while introducing them on the stage.

Not surprisingly, even fittingly, the lectures often focused on the theme of international leadership. This, of course, was in large part inspired by Sadat's legacy but also by the lives of the Sadat lecturers, who were all acknowledged leaders who received many distinctions, including the Nobel Prize for Peace that several shared with Anwar Sadat. I have spoken and written much about Sadat's leadership qualities that I witnessed closely, but some of the traits that stand out are a deep faith that provid-ed inner drive and a sense of destiny that prepared him to pay any price to do right.

The lectures span a decade of tumultuous change in the Middle East and in the relationship between the Middle East and the rest of the world. They mark important interpretations of events by some of the most accomplished and thoughtful practitioners of international relations: from Nelson Mandela's reflections on history and on the 9/11 tragedy, to Kofi Annan's articulation of the international role in pushing for Middle East peace, to Mary Robinson's discussion of human rights and racism, to George Mitchell's comparison of mediation in Ireland with mediation in the Middle East, to James Baker's articulation of the American role, to Mohamed ElBaradei's focus on human insecurity. Weizman, Carter, and Kissinger added richness with their own personal accounts of the Sadat years.

It has also been a true pleasure for me to be part of the Sadat Art for Peace Competition that accompanies the Sadat Lecture and that is generously supported by my friend Suzanne Cohen. This program has been truly inspiring. In cooperation with the outstanding Art Department at the University of

Maryland, the Sadat Chair for Peace and Development conducts a competition for the best sculpture and best flat art on the theme of peace. The sculpture is presented to the Sadat Lecturer, and the flat art is presented during the lecture and used for the cover of our lecture publication. Written reflections of the artists on the theme of their work also accompany the art. The works have been outstanding. One case was particularly memorable. A South African artist studying at the University of Maryland had produced the winning sculpture to present to Mandela. It was a superb piece that used some of the rocks from the South African prison where Mandela had served many difficult years. The accompanying reflections were so powerful that Mandela was visibly moved. When we suggested that we ship the sculpture to him in South Africa, he insisted that he carry it with him back home.

The Sadat Lectures are only part of the activities of the Sadat Chair for Peace and Development under the leadership of Professor Shibley Telhami, who has become a close friend. The University of Maryland has been particularly supportive, but I would like to thank a few special individuals who have been part of the effort of establishing the Sadat Chair and the Sadat Lectures. Chancellor William Kirwan, who was president when the chair was established, was an enthusiastic supporter from the beginning. President Mote, who arrived at Maryland in 1998, early enough to host the Carter lecture, has been actively encouraging and supportive. Irwin Goldstein, former dean of the College of Behavioral and Social Sciences, was always there when needed. His successor, Edward Montgomery, continued the tradition. Jonathan Wilkenfeld, former chair of the Department of Government and Politics that houses the Sadat Chair, and his successor, Mark Lichbach, have provided much support. Sapienza Barone of the Office of the University President was always indispensable in planning and carrying out the lecture with the able help of the Office of Special Events. I would also like to applaud the efforts of the Art Department in helping put together the Sadat Art for Peace Competition with encouragement from the dean of arts and humanities, James Harris.

What follows is a treat for all those interested in the theme of international peace, particularly in the Middle East, and certainly for those interested in Anwar Sadat and the legacy he left behind.

INTRODUCTION

A DECADE OF PERSPECTIVES ON PEACE

SHIBLEY TELHAMI

When Nelson Mandela delivered the Sadat Lecture for Peace at the University of Maryland on November 14, 2001, 10,000 people turned up to hear him, seeking comfort during a particularly painful period. The fall semester had started with the tragedy of 9/11 that all Americans endured. The College Park campus had experienced another tragedy of its own less than two weeks later when a rare tornado hit the community on September 24, 2001, killing two students, uprooting trees, damaging twelve buildings, and destroying and damaging 300 cars. All grief was briefly suspended for the healing experience of listening to the words of one of the greatest leaders of the twentieth century.

This was a particularly rewarding moment. When the Sadat Chair for Peace and Development was established at the University of Maryland in September 1997 and the Sadat Lectures conceived, Nelson Mandela was the type of leader the university aspired to host. The notion from the outset was to capture the responsibility of leadership in pursuing peace, exemplified by the role that Anwar Sadat had played, through a series of lectures by world leaders, especially those who had the kind of accomplishments that earned them global recognition, particularly winners of the Nobel Peace Prize. They were to be selected without regard to the ideological positions of the particular speakers.

From their beginning, the Sadat Lectures have not only been illuminating in their own right, but they have also provided an enlightening interpretation of a transformative period that saw the greatest hope that Arab-Israeli peace was within reach to the collapse of negotiations and the loss of faith in the prospects for peace. They have ranged from a period of almost unprecedented American leadership in the world to talk of the end of the American empire; from a period of economic prosperity for the United States and globally, with many singing the praises of globalization, to the type of economic crisis and decline that comes once in a century and brings fearful calls for protectionism. The 9/11 tragedy shook the world, and the American reaction launched two major wars and affected our lives and liberties at home.

The Sadat Lectures reflected the aftermath of these events, especially evident in Nelson Mandela's words and his gradually changing positions afterwards. Mandela was an unlikely supporter of President George W. Bush. But his meeting with the American president just before his Sadat Lecture and a few days after the Afghan war commenced showed the widespread sympathy and support the United States had received immediately after 9/11, even from states like Syria and Iran. At Maryland, Mandela described his position this way (see chapter 5):

> We have had occasion to express ourselves publicly in support of the current military actions by the United States and Britain in pursuit of those they identified as the perpetrators of the acts of terror. We accept that the United States and Britain are bent on bringing to book the identified terrorists and that the unfortunate civilian casualties that arise are coincidental. We accept that they will and are taking all precautions possible within a war situation to minimize civilian casualties and suffering.

Even in the face of criticism for siding with American action in Afghanistan, back in South Africa two weeks later Mandela continued to defend the United States: "I support the strikes against Afghanistan as far as it is intended to flush out Osama bin Laden. I have no sympathy with terrorists who kill 5,000 innocent civilians. I cannot tolerate that."[1] At the same time, he was beginning to warn that an attack on Iraq would be "disastrous." Within two weeks, his support for the Afghanistan war was giving way to concern about civilian casualties: "I never supported the bombing of the whole of Afghanistan and the killing of innocent children, elderly people, women and the disabled. I confined myself to bin Laden and his organization…."[2]

Mandela's position continued to evolve in a manner that reflected not only his own thinking but changing international attitudes. In January 2002—as American discourse became more strident after early successes in Afghanistan and talk increased about possible military action in Iraq—Mandela had second thoughts even about his early support for the Afghan war:

> Our view may have been one-sided and overstated . . . such unreserved support for the war in Afghanistan gives the impression that we are insensitive to and uncaring about the suffering inflicted upon the Afghan people and country . . . . Labeling of Osama bin Laden as the terrorist responsible for those acts before he has been tried and convicted could also be seen as undermining some of the basic tenets of the rule of law.[3]

But like many around the world, his biggest criticism of American policy was aimed at perceived American unilateralism as the United States geared up for the Iraq War. About a year after 9/11, in September 2002, Mandela stated, "We are really appalled by any country, whether it be a superpower or a small country, that goes outside the United Nations and attacks independent countries."[4] By January 2003, Mandela was increasingly frustrated by the American march toward the Iraq War, describing the U.S. stand on Iraq as "arrogant," and Mr. Bush as "a president who can't think properly and wants to plunge the world into holocaust."[5]

He had come full circle from the day he delivered the Sadat Lecture on November 14, 2001—as had much of the world.

The very fact that Nelson Mandela delivered the 2001 Sadat Lecture was itself driven by the 9/11 tragedy. At a time when then-Secretary of State Colin Powell was the leading advocate for American diplomacy on the Arab-Israeli conflict, the Sadat Chair had invited Secretary Powell to deliver the 2001 lecture. On September 10, 2001, the author received a phone call from then-Assistant Secretary of State William Burns to inform him the secretary of state had in principle accepted our invitation and asked him to pencil in a date in late September for Powell to deliver an important speech on Middle East peace policy at the University of Maryland. Within twenty-four hours, our national priorities were completely reshuffled.

That particular Powell lecture not given had a history of its own. A significantly modified version of Powell's prepared speech, altered to reflect the consequences of 9/11, was ultimately delivered as the Kentucky speech. By the time he delivered it, much had changed. The United States was embarked on a global war on terrorism that increasingly subsumed the Arab-Israeli conflict and redefined our national discourse. The events of September 11 also elevated the Department of Defense, as happens in times of war, to play the central role in the making of American foreign policy at the expense of the Department of State and Secretary Powell.

The Sadat Chair was inaugurated on October 7, 1997, with the first Sadat Lecture presented by then-President of Israel Ezer Weizman. Of all the Israeli politicians who had dealt with Anwar Sadat beginning with the Egyptian president's historic visit to speak at the Israeli Knesset in 1977, Weizman had a special place in Sadat's heart. Weizman's direct, casual ways and his personal warmth—and his comfort with Arab culture—earned him a close bond with the Egyptian leader that later translated into a special relationship with Egypt and Sadat's successor, President Hosni Mubarak. Weizman always felt that he could use this relationship to advance peace—but his effort was not always welcome in Israel.

Even as Weizman spoke at Maryland, tension was evident between him and his prime minister, Benjamin Netanyahu. As Weizman prepared to meet on his own with Egypt's president Hosni Mubarak a few weeks earlier, the planned meeting drew criticism from political sources close to Netanyahu.

"Through the meeting Egypt wants to use the president [Weizman] to assert the negative role it plays in the diplomatic process," one source reportedly said.[6] Although his position was largely ceremonial, Weizman had hoped that, as president, he could arrange for a formal, perhaps state-like dinner hosted by President Clinton at the White House. But strong objections from Prime Minister Netanyahu led to only a private dinner between the two presidents to which even Weizman's wife Reuma was not invited; Dr. Jehan Sadat and the University of Maryland arranged a private dinner for Mrs. Weizman at the Four Seasons Hotel while President Weizman met with President Clinton.

The personal tension between Weizman and Netanyahu indicated a rocky period in the peace process that the Oslo agreement between Israel and the Palestine Liberation Organization began in 1993. The most important breakthrough that the Oslo agreement achieved was psychological. The agreement created a widespread belief even among those who were not happy with its terms that the Palestinian-Israeli conflict was finally on its way to resolution. It also created alliances across the Israeli-Palestinian divide—and in the United States among those who pushed for peace. But the continued building of Jewish settlements in the West Bank, terrorist bombings in Israel, and the slow and contentious implementation of the agreement soured the mood among Israelis and Palestinians alike. The assassination of Israeli Prime Minister Yitzhak Rabin by an Israeli opposed to his peace moves changed the political picture in Israel and led to the election of Netanyahu—a man who had opposed the Oslo agreement. There was much tension in the region, with the Palestinians angry with limited Israeli withdrawals and Israelis confronting terrorist bombings inside Israel. There was also tension in the Israeli-American relationship.

Although President Weizman was welcome in the White House and admired for his forthcoming attitude in supporting the peace process, Prime Minister Netanyahu, who had angered White House officials by the tone of his conversation with President Clinton in his first visit to the White House, was less so. In the coming months, Clinton's anger with Netanyahu often translated into reluctance to respond to requests for meetings, even as the president was happy to meet with Palestinian leader Yasir Arafat. It was also in marked contrast to Clinton's attitude to Israeli Prime Minister Ehud Barak, who was elected two years later. Barak had unprecedented access to Clinton, both in person and by phone, in part due to Clinton's frustrations with the Netanyahu administration. He wanted to give Netanyahu's successor as much support as possible.

But the Netanyahu months were instructive about the U.S. relationship with Israel. A president who has the confidence of the Israeli public and of Americans who support Israel can be publicly at odds with the prime minister of Israel without losing much support—as long as there is a credible peace process on the table. Despite all the flaws of Oslo, most Americans, including supporters of Israel, believed that Oslo was the path to peace and that agreement in the end was inevitable. In that regard, Netanyahu was seen as an obstacle, creating much support for Clinton's approach. Tensions in the U.S.-Israeli relationship were probably one reason the Netanyahu government ultimately fell, giving rise to the Barak government.

Despite the tension and the short-term pessimism, like most analysts in the United States and the Middle East, in his Sadat Lecture Weizman expressed a sense of the inevitability of peace—and also of the significance of leadership in achieving it (see chapter 1):

> There are greater historians than I who believe that there are large currents in history and that it is just a matter of time until they occur. But originality of leadership is called for on the part of one leader or more to ride these historical waves in order to realize them. Otherwise, this moment of realization may move to a later period. And if it is correct to view history as a flowing river, it will continue to flow. . . . I am convinced that the Oslo Accords, which are to no small extent a continuation of the Camp David Accords on the Palestinian issue, will be put into effect.

If Weizman had a close relationship with Sadat, President Jimmy Carter was probably closer to the Egyptian president than any other world leader. In presenting the second Sadat Lecture in 1998, Carter was personal. After Sadat's first visit to the White House, Carter noted he felt "that a bright shining light came into my life with the visit of this singular man" (see chapter 2).

Carter's lecture was important as an intimate account of his personal relationship with Sadat and his role in the diplomacy leading to the Camp David Accords. It is striking that a president of the United States would take the kind of political risks that Carter did in elevating Arab-Israeli peacemaking in American priorities during a challenging period of the Cold War between the United States and the Soviet Union. Certainly, there were clear strategic benefits for the United States if it could achieve Egyptian-Israeli peace, reduce the influence of the Soviet Union, and decrease the prospect of Arab-Israeli wars. Carter and his chief advisers clearly understood these benefits. But there were also enormous risks.

For one thing, the history of the Arab-Israeli conflict is full of failed diplomacy. For another, although Carter was heartened by Sadat and his forthcoming leadership, he faced a new Israeli prime minister in Menachem Begin who was seen as ideological and uncompromising. If Benjamin Netanyahu was viewed later as a man with whom peace agreements with the Palestinians were less likely, the ascent of Begin as the first right-wing prime minister of Israel was historic and seemed to close the window for peaceful agreements. Carter's commitment and willingness to take risks, as he expressed in his lecture and elsewhere, were in part driven by his deep religious faith. But he was also encouraged by Sadat's attitude about Begin's election. Ideology aside, Sadat wanted to see a strong leader who could deliver and was prepared to take risks. The fact that an agreement was in the end concluded shows what may be possible with determined leadership. But the example is admittedly limited because Begin's most determined ideological commitments were in the West Bank, not the Sinai, and one of the benefits of concluding the deal with Egypt was to remove political and military leverage over Israel in the West Bank. Here, Carter was particularly hard on Begin because he believed that Begin mislead him on the important issue of freezing Jewish settlements in the West Bank.[7]

Consistent with his view on the possibility of making peace with seemingly hard-line leaders, Carter also surprisingly complimented Prime Minister Netanyahu (see chapter 2):

> Prime Minister Netanyahu is constrained I think by his own deep beliefs and also by his alliance with elements in Israeli political society that are more reluctant than he is to make steps to implement the Oslo agreement. And I think that he at Wye Plantation had to make the most courageous decision. It took a lot of courage which I admire deeply to make the concessions that Netanyahu has made.

That peacemaking can be politically risky, even when successful, was clear in Carter's remarks (see chapter 2). He believed that many Jewish Americans let him down because of the role he played. He put it this way:

> So I would say at the time we signed the peace treaty there was an almost unanimous favorable response, but over a period of time it dissipated. I would say in general the incumbent government of Israel draws support in this country from the Jewish community. And I think that is the way it ought to be. And that is probably the way I would feel if I were Jewish and were concerned about Israel being in danger. I think that makes negotiations very difficult. It made it difficult for me. It made it very difficult for President Reagan and Bush and now for President Clinton.

Carter was also critical of Arab allies in the quest for peace. In his lecture, he revealed that Saudi leaders had supported his efforts, even applauded them privately, only to criticize them publicly in a manner that made selling the Camp David Accords to the Arab world and preventing Egyptian isolation impossible. Carter disclosed the following in his Sadat Lecture (see chapter 2):

> Well, this in the past, I think, has been a secret that has not been known by anyone except me and then-Crown Prince Fahd, now King Fahd. Before we went to Camp David, I met with Crown Prince Fahd. He encouraged me to go and said he wished every success. When I left Israel in the spring of 1979 and flew to the airport in Cairo and got President Sadat's final approval of the exact text of the treaty and got into Air Force One to fly back to the States, the first message I got was from Saudi Arabia. It said: We are deeply pleased at the success you had and the peace treaty that we hope will bring an end of violence in our region. . . . So I can let you know that I had private assurances of encouragement from the Saudis to proceed. But publicly they joined in with other Arab leaders who objected.[8]

If President Carter and former Secretary of State Henry Kissinger had anything they agreed about passionately, it was their strong endorsement of, and friendship with, Anwar Sadat. When Kissinger delivered the Sadat Lecture for Peace in May 2000, the Clinton administration was intensely trying to broker an Israeli-Palestinian agreement in its last months in office. For the only time during any of the Sadat Lectures, students at the University of Maryland demonstrated against inviting Henry Kissinger to deliver a lecture on the theme of peace. The university's position was that the lectures should be diverse and the chair should invite prominent leaders who were appropriate for the theme of the lecture. Whether one agrees or disagrees with Kissinger, he was an important American decision-maker who was the first to deal closely with Anwar Sadat—and who also won the Nobel Peace Prize.

Kissinger, who described Sadat as the greatest man he had ever met in his diplomatic career, reviewed the historical context of his—and the American—relationship with Sadat. In particular, it is now clear that Sadat had made gestures toward the United States almost immediately after taking office after the death of his predecessor, President Gamal Abdel Nasser. Yet, the United States, and Kissinger in particular, did not take the Egyptian leader seriously until after the 1973 war and the subsequent Arab oil embargo. Was this a mistake? Could history have unfolded differently with an early American response? Kissinger put it this way (see chapter 3):

> I am quite frank to say that I did not understand Anwar Sadat when he first became president. Our intelligence reports described him as a weak man who had been put into that position because he could represent no conceivable threat to the president. And everyone expected two or three other leaders of Egypt to overthrow him at any moment. . . . Anwar Sadat made many threats, many statements, none of which, to my shame I must say, I took very seriously. Because it was absolutely axiomatic with us that there was no conceivable way that Egypt would dare to start a war.

If Henry Kissinger's lecture came during a time of intense American mediation of the Arab-Israeli conflict ultimately leading to the failed Camp David summit in July 2000, Senator George Mitchell's lecture was given in the midst of growing violence and pessimism about the prospects of Arab-Israeli peace. During the previous autumn, the second Palestinian Intifada had broken out with devastating consequences for Israelis and Palestinians from the terrorist attacks in Israel and the harsh Israeli operations in the Palestinian territories. President Clinton appointed Mitchell to investigate the developments and make recommendations. His report was ultimately submitted to President Bush in May 2001, just before he delivered the Sadat Lecture for Peace.

At that time, pessimism about the prospects of peace was in large part due to the collapse of the negotiations in July 2000 and to the subsequent outbreak of violence. But it is also clear that the Bush administration did not perceive the Arab-Israeli conflict to be central among American priorities, and it was particularly careful to differentiate its policies from those of the Clinton administration. In addition, it was no secret that many in the Arab world had preferred Bush over Al Gore in the American elections and expected him to be more responsive to their interests than the Clinton administration had been. Instead, it was clear early on that the Bush administration would fully support Sharon's government during a particularly violent period. Mitchell's was a welcome, clear-headed, judicious assessment that was badly needed internationally and in our national discourse.

Mitchell's lecture was notable in its careful comparison of his mediation in Northern Ireland with his mission in the Arab-Israeli arena. Although he saw many differences, the similarities were more striking, providing a sense of hope that, intractable as the Arab-Israeli issue may appear, in the end conflicts are started with people and end with people. He stressed his own source of patience and optimism in noting that mediation efforts almost always fail, sometimes in hundreds of attempts, but in the end one needs only one success. Coming in the middle of an otherwise gloomy picture of the prospects for peace, Mitchell's lecture was a notable exception.

Nelson Mandela's lecture came only a few weeks after the 9/11 tragedy. On November 13, 2002, Kofi Annan, then the secretary-general of the United Nations, became the second African leader to deliver the Sadat Lecture. This was a critical time in assessing the role of the United Nations because the Bush administration seemed determined to wage war against the Iraqi government of Saddam Hussein—even if unilaterally. For example, during that same week, the author published *The Stakes: America and the Middle East* (Boulder, Colo.: Westview Press, 2002), which emphasized the risks of unilateralism, the crucial nature of the Arab-Israeli conflict, and potential detrimental consequences of war in Iraq. The Kofi Annan lecture and its theme were certainly timely.

Annan, like other Sadat lecturers, saw the late Egyptian president as a symbol for leadership and for understanding the importance of psychology in transforming political choices, and he noted how being a strong leader sometimes means going against conventional wisdom (See chapter 6):

> By all conventional wisdom, he should not have done what he did. Going to Jerusalem, with no assurance in advance of any concessions from the other side, seemed to almost all Arabs at the time an act of folly, if not outright treason. Yet President Sadat understood the vital importance of psychology in war and peace. He understood that political behavior is deeply influenced by the mental image that each side has of the other—and that sometimes this image can only be changed by an act of breathtakingly radical daring.

In his review of the requirements for peace for both Israelis and Palestinians, Annan positively cited the Saudi peace plan that was endorsed by the Arab summit conference in Beirut in March 2002. He projected empathy for both sides, articulating their hopes and fears, and ending by emphasizing an international role to help shatter the barriers of suspicion, fear, and rejection—without proposing any specific steps.

Former Secretary of State James A. Baker III provided a unique perspective during a difficult time in Arab-Israeli peacemaking. As a Republican supporter of President George W. Bush and his administration, he nonetheless presented views on the issues that were at odds with the Bush administration's policy. Baker had considerable experience in dealing with the Arab-Israeli issue and the Middle East more broadly. As secretary of state during the administration of George H. W. Bush, he played a vital role in putting together the international coalition to force Iraq out of Kuwait and raising the funds for the effort from international sources, in an episode that is considered one of the major American foreign policy successes of recent decades. He was the force behind the Madrid Conference that brought Arabs and Israelis to the negotiating table after the war and also involved the Palestinians and the Syrians for the first time. In historical perspective, Baker's diplomacy is seen to be among the most successful in American policy in the past two decades.[9] His view during a difficult period was important.

In his Sadat Lecture, Baker praised President George W. Bush for his action to remove Saddam Hussein and for his stated policy of spreading democracy in the Middle East. But Baker called for more aggressive Middle East diplomacy and put forth one of the clearest statements presented in any of the lectures on the basic components of Arab-Israeli peace. The details of the steps he articulated and the American role in carrying them out deserve close attention. Addressing the planned Israeli withdrawal from Gaza, he warned that "the administration must make it unambiguously clear to Israel that although Prime Minister Sharon's planned withdrawal from Gaza is a positive initiative, it cannot be simply the first step in a unilateral process leading to the creation of Palestinian Bantustans in the West Bank" (see chapter 8).

Although noting that the United States cannot create peace in the Middle East, Baker declared that "it is clear that the United States must and will continue to play a key role in the Middle East, and we have a variety of tools to address the challenges presented there" (see chapter 8).

Mary Robinson was the first European leader to deliver the Sadat Lecture—as well as the first woman. She was well known for her effective leadership as president of Ireland and also for her role as the United Nations human rights commissioner. She was widely recognized as a passionate advocate of human rights and continued her work in that area after leaving the United Nations.

But Robinson was clearly surprised by the perception that her leadership at the UN was marked by a period of anti-Israel sentiment. Much of that perception came out of the Durban Conference, which was critical of Israeli actions in the Palestinian territories and which was held under her leadership. As a tough fighter against racism and anti-Semitism, Robinson felt that she was misunderstood and that her role in Durban, South Africa, was also misrepresented. She put it this way, "At a conference in which we were supposed to be defending human rights values, we found ourselves faced with appalling bigotry and intolerance. I and many others condemned such language and, in the circumstances, I refused to recommend the final NGO document to the conference" (see chapter 7). It was with this background that she gave her lecture. It was simultaneously a lecture for peace and one that denounced racism and anti-Semitism.

Speaking on Saint Patrick's Day 2004, Robinson reflected on the peacemaking efforts in Northern Ireland and situated the pursuit of Middle East peace in broader human and global contexts (see chapter 7).

> The title I have chosen for my address is "The Journey to Peace: Finding Ourselves in the Other." It reflects what, for me, was President Sadat's great insight as a leader. He understood in reaching out to the people of Israel that he was reaching out not so much to a different nation or culture, but to a shared human desire for acceptance, security and dignity.

When Mohamed ElBaradei delivered the Sadat Lecture, there was much focus on his work in his capacity as director general of the International Atomic Energy Agency (IAEA)—for which he had won the Nobel Prize for peace. He had felt vindicated after the Iraq War, when it turned out that Iraq had no weapons of mass destruction and that, as his agency had noted before the war, its nuclear program had ended many years earlier. Nonetheless, there was no hiding the fact that his relationship with the Bush administration had been tense from the days of disagreement over Iraq and concerns that disagreements were emerging in the way the IAEA and its director were dealing with the Iranian nuclear program.

Dr. ElBaradei was the first Egyptian to deliver the lecture and to reflect on his former president's legacy. He provided a perspective on what the Egyptian president sought to achieve and why his vision remains unfulfilled. Although he also talked about nuclear proliferation, he placed the issue in the context of a broader notion of peace. His basic proposition was that, "Conventional concepts of security—rooted in the protection of national borders and old concepts of sovereignty—are no longer adequate. . . . The modern age demands that we think in terms of *human* security—a concept of security that is people-centered and without borders." Dr. ElBaradei described his expanded notion of human insecurity (see chapter 9):

> Statistics indicate that the world is becoming more peaceful. Yet at the same time, the collective sense of insecurity is higher than at any time before because the forces that drive insecurity remain persistent and pervasive. These drivers of insecurity fit into four categories: First, poverty, and poverty-related insecurities. . . . A second category is the lack of good governance. . . which ranges from corruption to severely repressive regimes whose hallmark is egregious human rights abuses. . . . A third driver of insecurity is the sense of injustice that results from the imbalance between the haves and have-nots. . . . Fourth is the artificial polarization along religious or ethnic lines. . . . The human security picture would not be complete without factoring in the impact of globalization. . . .

Like other Sadat lecturers, Mohamed ElBaradei emphasized the role of leadership in international politics and described President Sadat's visit to Jerusalem as "a leap of faith to shatter deeply entrenched psychological barriers of fear, distrust and rejection" (see chapter 9).

Because many Sadat Lectures focused on the role of leadership and particularly the role of the United States, I asked a former American diplomat, Aaron David Miller, who had written about both leadership and American foreign policy, to write a concluding chapter reflecting on the Sadat Lectures, Sadat's legacy, and American diplomacy in the Middle East.

So much has changed in the past decade in the Middle East and in its relations with the United States—and yet so much has not. The discourse remains focused on Jewish settlements, occupation, and terrorism. Benjamin Netanyahu—who was prime minister of Israel when the University of Maryland inaugurated the Sadat Lecture for Peace but whose career seemingly abruptly ended two years later—returned to play the same role in Israeli politics after about a decade. Ariel Sharon—whose prospects for political comeback seemed over in 1982 after his indirect role in the massacre of Palestinians at Sabra and Shatila, returned as a powerful prime minister—led Israeli forces out of Gaza. Sharon's subsequent ill health has created a vacuum of leadership in Israel, one that has brought back to prominence both Ehud Barak and Netanyahu.

Senator George Mitchell, who gave a Sadat Lecture as a special envoy for President Clinton, has returned as the special Middle East envoy of President Obama and Secretary of State Hillary Clinton. Many of the same leaders, or their sons, are still in charge in the Arab world. The most consequential change may have been the division among the Palestinians into two competing centers of power, one led by Hamas and the other by Fatah. The two-state solution that seemed inevitable in 1997 appears more at risk than at any time since the Oslo agreement. Stable alternatives that are fair and acceptable to both sides are hard to see, and a collapse of the two-state solution may entail protracted conflict for another generation of Arabs and Israelis, with challenges for American foreign policy.

Yet, in reviewing a decade of perspectives on peace by many of those who helped write international history over the past several decades, there are two striking conclusions. The first is that peace agreements are often reached when unanticipated and by those who seemingly are incapable of producing them, which suggests that diplomacy should not be deterred by short-term political shifts, even as it must take careful account of them. Second, leadership is often essential in creating change, and the example Anwar Sadat set made the theme of leadership central to the Sadat Lectures. This was particularly so in the case of the three lecturers who knew him best—Carter, Weizman, and Kissinger.

But leadership is hard to define and even harder to anticipate. Leadership is often associated with profound historical change, which by definition is difficult to foresee. Social scientists are trained to predict events by projecting patterns of the past into the future. Yet profound change is a break from the very past that guides the work of scholars. And leadership is frequently the unknown factor that accounts for change.

Although the Sadat lecturers universally hailed the acts of leadership of Anwar Sadat, what they meant by leadership is hard to pin down. Some often mean courage, which entails a leader's willingness to take political or even personal risk. But where does one draw the boundaries between courage and recklessness? Is it wisdom when leaders ignore their advisers or public opinion based on their own convictions? Mature democracies work hard to limit the possibility that any particular leader will have a free hand to act on behalf of the state and to produce systemic checks and balances that ensure such limitations. Carter, a friend and admirer of Sadat's, reflected on and even criticized the Egyptian leader's independence. He put it this way in answering a question from the audience: "Sadat was, I think, overly immune to the condemnation of those within the Arab world who disagreed with him. I used to argue with him about that. He was impervious to this, which may be one of the causes of his assassination" (see chapter 2).

The ultimate historical judgment of leadership seems mostly based on interpreting the consequences of leaders' actions. Whether George W. Bush was a great leader, a reckless gambler, or a man of vision or of baseless convictions in taking the United States to war in Iraq will ultimately be based on—more than anything else—the historical judgment of the consequences of that war. It will also matter who will be judging because the consequences will differ across countries and peoples.

In Sadat's case, such differences explain why his legacy has been mixed depending on those affected by his actions. For many in Egypt, Israel, the West, and other countries around the world, he was a hero for the boldness of his actions that brought about an Egyptian-Israeli peace that has endured for the past three decades. But many in the Arab world saw in his actions weakness and increasing dependence on the United States, as well as consequences that weakened the hand of Arabs, particularly the Palestinians, in relation to Israel. At the same time, these interpretations of Sadat's leadership were historically fluid: When hopes increased after the Oslo agreement between Israel and the Palestinians that the type of comprehensive peace to which Sadat aspired was within reach, Sadat's popularity in Egypt and parts of the Arab world grew. After the negotiations collapsed in July 2000, the number of Arabs who judged him harshly increased. His ultimate legacy will always be connected to the extent to which a comprehensive peace in the Middle East is seen to have been served or delayed.

Beyond the theme of leadership, many of the lecturers addressed notions of comprehensive peace—not only in the Middle Eastern context but also conceptually. At one level, many of the lectures were specific to the Middle East, and in that context articulated what it would take to reach a stable, comprehensive peace in the region, encompassing Israel and all its neighbors—and beyond. A number of lecturers—including Kofi Annan, Nelson Mandela, and Mohamed ElBaradei—offered broad ideas on this issue. Former American Secretary of State

James Baker (who was the architect of a regional approach to peacemaking in the Madrid process that followed the 1991 Iraq War) presented a detailed plan for moving forward toward a far-reaching peace in the region while avoiding being especially critical of the administration of George W. Bush, who was president at the time of Baker's lecture.

Another sense of comprehensive peace, however, is conceptual. Mohamed ElBaradei spoke of the need not only to reduce the prospect of major war but also to reduce a persistent and pervasive sense of insecurity, which, in his mind, is often a function of poverty, poor governance, an imbalance between the haves and have nots, and "the artificial polarization along religious and ethnic lines."

Nelson Mandela also addressed the need for a comprehensive peace in the Middle East but, speaking only weeks after 9/11, inevitably articulated the need to confront terrorism and tied it in part to addressing global poverty. Former UN Secretary-General Kofi Annan understandably linked his views of Middle Eastern peace to international law and UN resolutions. Mary Robinson, a former UN human rights commissioner, centered her views of international peace and human security on notions of human rights.

A third theme in many of the lectures pertains specifically to the role of the United States of America in achieving Middle East peace. This was perhaps inevitable, given that Sadat's primary foreign policy achievement, the Camp David accords, could not have happened without the crucial role of President Jimmy Carter. Sadat himself believed that most of the cards pertaining to Middle East peace were in the hands of the United States. And four of the Sadat lecturers (Carter, Kissinger, Baker, and Mitchell) were American leaders who worked on Arab-Israeli peace. Aaron David Miller's concluding chapter also focuses on the American role, made even more timely with the advent of the Obama administration, which started off by appointing an American envoy, Senator George Mitchell, to mediate Arab-Israeli peace.

Although scholars and American officials have often debated how crucial the American role in bringing about peace in the Middle East is and also how important the pursuit of peace is to American interests, it is notable that American leaders who delivered the Sadat lecture have all been involved in successful diplomacy. Despite the ideological and intellectual differences among the four American lecturers (two Republicans and two Democrats) about effective diplomacy and the American role—all were deeply involved in the successful episodes. Henry Kissinger, who describes his deep involvement in the negotiations but who at various times did not see a need for American engagement, succeeded in negotiating disengagement of forces agreements between Israel on the one hand and Egypt and Syria on the other only when the United States elevated Middle East diplomacy in its priorities after the 1973 Arab-Israeli War (even as President Nixon was consumed by the Watergate scandal).

Carter gave the Middle East considerable attention even before Sadat undertook his visit to Jerusalem but emphasized the issue even more after that visit. And Baker, with the full support of President George H. W. Bush, initiated the Madrid process only after the United States decided to make the Middle East a priority after the 1991 Iraq War.

In the end, one should keep in mind that many of the Sadat lecturers were telling the story of events in which they participated. Their involvement lends much credibility to the accounts presented, but it is always important to remember that leaders often recall facts differently in retrospect, and that there is a context that must be understood in evaluating these events.

In Carter's case, for example, his accounts are obviously important and authoritative. He strongly believes that the prime minister of Israel, Menachem Begin, misled him or violated his pledge to him on the settlement issue, as mentioned above. There are, of course, other accounts by the Israelis and important clarifications by scholars such as William Quandt, who participated in the Camp David negotiations. Carter also believed that the Saudis reneged on their promised support for the Camp David Accords, based on direct communications he received from Saudi leaders. But it may well be the case that the Saudis' initial understanding of what was actually agreed turned out to be inaccurate, particularly on the issues of Israeli settlements and the degree of association between the proposed Palestinian autonomy and the Egyptian-Israeli peace treaty.

In the lectures to follow, and in the concluding chapter, there is much to ponder about the indispensable role of leadership in the events of the last several decades in the Middle East and in the role of the United States in that region. These lectures provide a tribute to one particular leader, Anwar Sadat, who impressed both those who agreed and those who disagreed with him with his boldness and courage in acting to transform political possibilities.

Notes

1. "Mandela warns against Iraq strikes," *BBC World News,* December 3, 2001, http://news.bbc.co.uk/2/low/africa/1690041.stm (accessed October 23, 2008).

2. "Mandela heckled at mosque for supporting war," *The Star,* December 13, 2001, http://www.iol.co.za/general/newsview.php?art_id=ct20011213211361448U23219&click_id=13&set_id=1 (accessed October 23, 2008).

3. Henri E. Cauvin, "A NATION CHALLENGED: SOUTH AFRICA; In Statement, Mandela Shifts on All-Out Support for War," *New York Times,* January 3, 2002, http://query.nytimes.com/gst/fullpage.html?res=9C01E0D91330F930A35752C0A9649C8B63 (accessed October 23, 2008).

4. "Mandela calls Bush to Talk about Iraq," *Dispatch Online,* September 3, 2002, http://www.dispatch.co.za/2002/09/03/southafrica/AAAALEAD.HTM (accessed October 23, 2008).

5. "Mandela condemns US stance on Iraq," *BBC World News,* January 30, 2003, http://news.bbc.co.uk/2/hi/africa/2710181 (accessed October 23, 2008).

6. "Weizman and Mubarak Aim to Break Ice," *Turkish Daily News,* May 23, 2997, http://www.hurriyetdailynews.com/h.php?news=weizman-and-mubarak-aim-to-break-ice-1997005-23 (accessed on October 24, 2008).

7. It should be noted that Begin never accepted Carter's version and that there are a number of different interpretations of what happened at Camp David. For an authoritative account, see William Quandt, *Camp David: Peacemaking and Politics* (Washington, D.C.: Brookings Institution, 1986).

8. The Saudis may have misunderstood the exact terms of the agreement. In particular, it is clear that two specific issues were the most important to them and other Arabs: linking the Egyptian-Israeli agreement and the agreement on Palestinian autonomy and an enforceable freeze on Jewish settlements in the Palestinian territories. The absence of these was a major factor in the decision of many Arab governments to oppose the Camp David Accords.

9. The work of James Baker during the George H. W. Bush administration received high marks in a study of nearly twenty years of diplomacy in the Arab-Israeli conflict by three American administrations. The study was published by the United States Institute of Peace as *Negotiating Arab-Israeli Peace: American Leadership in the Middle East,* by Daniel Kurtzer and Scott Lasensky, with Steven Spiegel, William Quandt, and Shibley Telhami (Washington, D.C.: United States Institute of Peace Press, 2007).

1

EZER WEIZMAN

I am pleased to be visiting here today and to be giving the first lecture in memory of the late president of Egypt, my friend, Anwar Sadat, as part of the Sadat Chair program.

I have come here today to pay tribute to the cause of peace and to the brave persons who relentlessly worked so hard in trying to achieve it.

There are greater historians than I who believe that there are large currents in history and that it is just a matter of time until they occur. But originality of leadership is called for on the part of one leader or more to ride these historical waves in order to realize them. Otherwise, this moment of realization may move to a later period. And if it is correct to view history as a flowing river, it will continue to flow.

Twenty years ago, in 1977–78, we found ourselves at a time of three strong and significant leaders who headed the elements influencing the flow of history in our region. Prime Minister Menachem Begin and President Anwar Sadat, may their souls rest in peace, and President Jimmy Carter. The three of them aspired to reach an agreement, each of them—I do not know this for a fact, but I do have a firm basis for believing so—for his own reasons.

With the end of the Yom Kippur War, and particularly in 1975, following the signing of the second Disengagement of Forces Agreement with Egypt, a new era began in the Middle East. It continues to this very day and focuses on the attempts to achieve peace. In this era of aspiration for peace, a number of significant events have occurred. The United States has been an active partner in all of them. The main and most exciting event was twenty years ago, when President Sadat visited Israel in November 1977.

The second most significant event happened in 1993, here in Washington, on the White House lawn. It was the historic handshake of the late Israeli Prime Minister, Yitzhak Rabin, with the chairman of the Palestine Liberation Organization, Yasir Arafat. It took place under the auspices of the president of the United States of America, Bill Clinton.

There are clear lines of similarity between Anwar Sadat's historic act in coming to Jerusalem and Yitzhak Rabin's historic act in shaking Arafat's hand. Both Sadat and Rabin understood that one has to grab the moment and to rise above personal feelings, above memories of the past, above the expected opposition at home, and perform an act that for them personally was very difficult at the time. They did so out of a correct reading of the situation and with foresight.

These two great leaders, Sadat and Rabin, paid with their lives for their actions. They fell for the sake of peace. Both were gunned down by religious zealots who were afraid of progress and who wanted to turn the Middle East back to the past.

Another significant event that has to be mentioned occurred in 1995, in the Israeli-Jordanian Arava desert, namely the signing of a peace treaty between Israel and the Kingdom of Jordan.

The Oslo Accords and the peace treaty with Jordan would never have occurred had it not been for the peace treaty with Egypt.

I would like to tell you something about President Sadat. At the many meetings I had with him, I found an unusual man. He spoke about the future with the confidence of someone who could actually see it. For me, the peace process with Egypt was complex. It was strange to sit with a leader of an enemy country and, after some time, to reach an understanding and a common denominator with him. I had never even imagined that such a thing could happen to me. I learned from him a few things that to us, the Israelis, were unclear. For example, that Egypt was the leader of the Arab world. More than once I heard him say that there will be no war and no peace without Egypt. I also sensed that he felt himself to be an integral part of the people. He in-

timated to me more than once that he saw Mubarak as his successor, as he wanted what he started to continue after him. From this point of view, he was successful, because President Mubarak, with all the difficulties, continues to favor the peace process and tries to promote it.

In the lengthy talks that we had, I also understood that Egypt's leadership would not be satisfied with a bilateral peace between Israel and Egypt but that the Palestinian issue also had to be resolved. A solution to the Palestinian matter was a necessary factor for overall peace with the Arab world. And so indeed it was. Menachem Begin, who, like so many of us, favored a Greater Israel, recognized the legitimate rights of the Palestinian people by adding his signature to the Camp David Accords. In the bonds that were formed between Sadat and myself, and between his wife Jehan and my wife Reuma, we also got to know members of his family and the warmth he gave and the importance he attached to them.

Let me try and explain the background that led to the peace talks between Israel and Egypt. From my many meetings with President Sadat, I came to realize that at the beginning of the 1970s he wanted to escape from Soviet influence and replace it with American. There was no great love between the Egyptian regime and the Soviet advisers in Egypt.

It would be an understatement to say that Sadat did not like the Soviet presence in Egypt. He once told me that a year before the Yom Kippur War, he had instructed them to leave Egypt. He asked them to leave within two weeks, and they left within ten days . . . and the whole war (he added with undisguised pride) was waged under Egyptian command.

A second point was Sadat's desire to break the political ice. This was in fact one of his aims when he went to war in 1973. He had no intention of conquering the state of Israel, but he certainly had the intention of inflicting a painful blow on us, and this he did. After the Yom Kippur War, he put it into words: "Now I can speak with a clear conscience toward my people." He crossed the Suez Canal and took a foothold on the eastern side. Despite Israel's success in encircling the Third Army, the first Disengagement of Forces Agreement resulted in Egyptian forces remaining east of the canal and, in the course of time, to its reopening.

I imagine that, following these achievements, he said to himself, "Now I am ready to talk to the Israelis." And this he did.

To these points should be added, of course, the economic and demographic situation of Egypt, of which Sadat was always aware. He looked for ways to change it from its foundations.

On the other side was Menachem Begin. The year 1977 was the first time since the establishment of the state of Israel that a man of the right was elected to its leadership. A large part of the public was convinced that if a person such as he were to come to power, he would take us back to the cycle of war. I do not examine innermost thoughts, but I guess that, apart from his burning desire for peace—and that is the complete truth—Begin also wanted to prove that he, of all people, an out-and-out right-winger, would be the one to bring peace. And so he agreed to welcome President Sadat in Jerusalem.

Regarding the third leader, President Jimmy Carter, I have more evaluations than facts. First, there is a clear American interest for peace and quiet in the Middle East, both because of the sources of oil and, no less important, because of the Suez Canal. Closure of the canal doubled and tripled the price of oil. Another factor, which is perhaps of prime importance, is that Carter is a religious man. His desire for peace stemmed from his belief that it was his duty to bring peace to the children of Abraham, as he put it. It is a fact that Carter devoted much time, thought, and effort to attaining peace in the Middle East.

There is one more thing that I must add. On the internal political level in Israel, the opposition of the Labor Party made a wide common denominator possible. I don't think we could have reached unanimity of 100 percent because democracy by its nature divides rather than unites. But in important moments, when historical decisiveness is possible, one has to aspire for a maximum common denominator, and that was achieved in 1978.

At the beginning, the meetings between Israel and Egypt were good and moving, but already on his historical visit to Jerusalem, Sadat gave a speech that was very difficult for us Israelis to digest. About a month later, we set off for Ismailia, Prime Minister Menachem Begin, Foreign Minister Moshe Dayan, and myself, minister of defense, as well as our aides and advisers. There we found a president facing a prime minister, ministers facing ministers, one group facing the other, and we sat down to cope with the serious problems. It was winter then in Ismailia, but in the room it was rather hot. We sat in a closed room. The tension rose. Begin started to bring examples of peace treaties from the past. I saw Sadat wipe the perspiration from his forehead with a handkerchief.

I already knew him somewhat by then, and I realized that he was tense. Begin continued his lengthy talk, quoting from a book by an expert on international law, when suddenly Sadat clapped his hands. One of the attendants then entered the room. *"Iftah ishubak"* (open the window), Sadat commanded. "He's very tense," I whispered to Begin. "So am I," he replied tersely.

The meeting at Ismailia ended, one might say, without undue success. But the meetings continued. In the following months, I traveled to Egypt fifteen times. Moshe Dayan did, too, and he also met with Egyptians in England. There were crises. Moods of disappointment began to sweep through the Israeli public, which had put so much hope in the negotiations. And then Carter moved—it might have been a one-time act that would not be repeatable—and invited us to Camp David, with the explicit request that no one would leave the place until an agree-

ment was reached. (It must be added that Camp David is not a prison; one has everything there—a swimming pool, cinema, sport facilities—and the conditions are certainly comfortable, all here in the state of Maryland). I imagine that President Carter thought that if he could convene us all together under one roof, eventually white smoke would emerge.

By then it was already clear to us that Sadat was vehemently insisting on the return of the whole of Sinai. The hope that we might be able to retain something (the settlements of Pithat Rafiah, Sharm el-Sheikh) was quickly shelved. Both Moshe Dayan and I had been in the military for decades and had fought against Egypt more than once. In 1948 during the War of Independence, I had attacked the Egyptian army's columns between Ashdod and Yavneh, about 30 km from Tel Aviv. Therefore, a very strong mental effort was needed to come to Camp David with a new perception of the situation that differed from the one we had developed in the army. In addition, it was clear to us that Sadat's intention was not just a bilateral agreement between Israel and Egypt but an agreement in which the Palestinian issue would be included. Something should be mentioned here that people tend to forget: the Camp David agreement was a framework agreement for peace among Israel and Egypt, Syria, Jordan, Lebanon, and the Palestinians. Matters such as the removal of settlements featured in it. Before we set out, Begin summarized at a cabinet meeting the subject of the autonomy that was to be offered to the Palestinians.

After twelve difficult and tense days at Camp David, the agreement was signed. In principle, it determined a return to international borders, a return of the Israeli settlers to Israel (it did not refer to the removal of settlements but to a return of people), and, of course, diplomatic relations and normalization among the countries.

The agreement set milestones for the autonomy. Everyone understood that the autonomy was supposed to be an interim situation of three to five years, before the final status was to be resolved, including the borders. The autonomy, therefore, did not feature as a permanent solution but as an interim stage before the permanent arrangement. (We were very careful not to use the terrible expression "final solution"). It was decided not to include a number of issues in the document but to send letters about them to the United States. One of the most prominent of these was the issue of Jerusalem. Begin, in his letter, had declared Jerusalem to be one indivisible city. Sadat did agree that essential functions in the city should be undivided, and a joint municipal council composed of an equal number of Arab and Israeli members can supervise the carrying out of these functions.

The second issue of importance that was raised in the exchange of letters was the evacuation of the Israeli settlers from Sinai. Begin announced in his letter that evacuation of settlers would be condi-tional on agreement being reached on all the outstanding matters, namely only as the final subject. He was furious when it was published that he had easily agreed to concede on that matter and reemphasized that it would be decided only by a Knesset vote and that coalition members of the Knesset would be given freedom to vote as they wished on this matter.

Begin was torn on the matter of the settlements. I have no doubt as to his integrity, when he said in the Knesset debate, "With a heavy and grieving heart but with a clear conscience, I will recommend [evacuation of the settlements] because this is the way that leads to peace." As he spoke, I could almost hear his heart break.

And then a difficult process began, one of tiring discussions about various sections. Moshe Dayan and I stayed at the Madison Hotel, here in Washington, facing Boutros-Ghali, the deputy foreign minister, and Kamal Hassan Ali, the minister of defense. After negotiating and arguing, in the end, we again needed Jimmy Carter to close the gaps. On March 26, 1979, on the White House lawn, we signed the first peace agreement between Israel and an Arab country.

There are those who will say that we should have stood firm, not given in, not conceded, and not moved. I don't think so. The greatness of leaders is measured in their ability to shake free of slogans, of their standing orders, of opinions that have been left behind and to understand the historical currents.

And that was the greatness of Anwar Sadat, Menachem Begin, and Jimmy Carter, as witnessed at Camp David.

In the last four years since the signing of the Oslo Accords, we have gone a long way with the Palestinians. There have been many obstacles and many difficulties, including very serious attacks against the civilian population in Israel, causing grave damage to the national morale. We are now in a very complex crisis between us and the Palestinian leadership with which we signed an agreement. This crisis is also causing a worsening of relations between us and Egypt and Jordan.

Over the years, we have gone through a difficult and ongoing war in Lebanon, along Israel's northern border. On this issue, I fully believe that, without an agreement with Syria, we will not have peace and quiet in Lebanon, as Syria is a key country in the Middle East.

I permit myself, from this podium, to call upon President Assad and the leaders of other Arab countries to join the long journey that President Sadat started.

The attacks on the Israeli population are very severe, and the two sides are in a crisis of mistrusting each other. But, despite the tribulations, the troubles, and the killings that the people of Israel have faced, we must not lose faith. At the same time, we have to ensure that any political solution will contain within it components of security, both general and personal.

It must be recalled that, when one talks about the final status of the Palestinian issue, one is also talking about the permanent status of the state of Israel. And it is worth stating here, both to my people and to the Palestinian people, that we need not receive everything and they will not receive everything. In the final resort, we will find ourselves drawing a map with borders on which will be determined what is ours and what is theirs.

Just as Sadat wanted cooperation between Egypt and Israel, so we, too, have to attain cooperation between the Palestinians and Israel today. I am certain that the prime minister of Israel, Benjamin Netanyahu, who is committed to the Oslo Accords, will do and is doing his utmost to promote cooperation between us and the Palestinians. The subject of peace is at the top of the national list of priorities for the prime minister of Israel, and I am sure that he and the government of Israel will realize the aims of the government by establishing peace and security with the Palestinians and with all our neighbors.

I prefer a satisfied neighbor, living a peaceful life, to a dissatisfied one. Just as President Carter, with his strength and wisdom, promoted the peace between Egypt and ourselves and the first buds of a solution of the Palestinian issue, so President Clinton was best man of the Oslo Accords. He promoted and was a partner in the peace treaty with Jordan, and it is clear that the influence and power of the United States of America, on the same lines as twenty years ago, led to the Oslo Accords. I am convinced that the Oslo Accords, which are to no small extent a continuation of the Camp David Accords on the Palestinian issue, will be put into effect.

President Sadat's first, brave step for peace meant that he was unpopular in the Arab world but, with time, the recognition grew amongst some of the Arabs of the merit of joining this path. There are currently four partners in the process—Israel, Egypt, Jordan, and the Palestinians—and they are so deeply involved in the process that they would really have to be insane to pull out of it. Even though a new misfortune occurs almost daily, everything has to be done to prevent us from being dragged into a war of a religious extremist nature.

I hope that the currents of history are stronger than anything else and that they will overcome the crises and we will succeed in achieving arrangements that will ensure us and our children of a secure and true peace in the Middle East.

It is the duty of all, and of all the parties involved, to continue believing in peace and to do our utmost to attain peace in our region.

In conclusion, I should like to thank you, sir, the president, the administration, and the faculty of the university for honoring me today on this auspicious occasion with the honorary degree of Doctor of the University of Maryland.

And finally, to a good lady and my friend, Dr. Jehan Sadat, I want to pay my respects for your tireless efforts to carry on the legacy of your great husband.

2

JIMMY CARTER

In thinking about what I was going to say today, I decided not to write a text but just to reminisce about some of the things that have been important to me in dealing with this vitally important subject.

But I came today not because of entreaties, not because of my respect for Jehan Sadat, and not even because of my respect for this great university. I came for a different purpose and wanted to come last year. The first year I was in office, I met sixty-eight foreign leaders, some who came to the White House on formal occasions and others when I visited the United Nations in New York. And in the next three years I met a number of others. This is my seventeenth year as a professor at Emory University. I have given a lot of lectures in that time, and I have been asked a lot of questions. One of the most frequent questions is: Who is the greatest leader you have ever met in your life? And I have only had one answer: President Anwar Sadat of Egypt.

I first met Anwar Sadat just a few months after I became president. I had taught Sunday school for many years—I taught this morning before I left my home—and I had a deep religious interest in the Holy Land. I had learned as a candidate and as a new president the importance of the Middle East to me personally, to those who share faith in God, and to those who are concerned about the integrity and the future peace of my own country.

There was an alignment of forces in the Middle East that was very disturbing. The powerful Soviet Union in the depths of the Cold War aligned with certain groups, and our country aligned with others. I felt it incumbent upon me to cast aside any restraints regarding political popularity or the risk of failure and began to seek a way to bring peace to the region. I began to meet with Middle East leaders. I was distressed when I met with then-Prime Minister Rabin of Israel, who was extremely cautious. I then met with King Hussein of Jordan, President Assad from Syria, and Crown Prince Fahd from Saudi Arabia. It was not encouraging, the totality of it.

Then President Anwar Sadat came to meet with me. We had our normal conference—one side filled with Americans and the other with Egyptians—followed by a banquet in the evening with some entertainment. Afterwards I felt a strange rapport with that man that has been almost unequaled in my life. I invited Anwar to go upstairs with me, to a place in the White House where very few people visit, to the second floor where the families live. He went up with me. Our little daughter Amy was asleep, and I woke her up and said, "Amy, I want you to meet a new friend." And President Sadat met my daughter. We then went and sat on the corner of a sofa, and I began to explain to him my dreams of peace in the Middle East. I found a receptivity that I had not experienced anywhere else, and I began to recognize the attributes that made him great. He was calm, self-assured, and had a far-sighted awareness of global interrelatedness. It was obvious that he was bold and did not lack political courage. We explored some ideas. There were some things he said would never happen in his lifetime. He said we might see Israeli ships going through the Suez Canal, but there would never be an exchange of ambassadors.

After he left, I knew—and made a public statement saying—that a bright shining light came into my life with the visit of this singular man. I asked Anwar Sadat to help me break the ice that had frozen over as a result of four wars between Egypt and Israel in the last twenty-five years. Later, when I had not made any progress after a very conservative Menachem Begin was elected prime minister of Israel, Sadat said he would like to do something that was bold. I encouraged him. His first thought was to invite the five permanent members of the United Nations Security Council to come together to promote peace in the Middle East. I said there

was no way to invite all five—the United States, Soviet Union, China, France, and Great Britain—that it would just complicate the issue.

We exchanged ideas again, and in September he said that he would be willing to go to Jerusalem. He announced this publicly after he had consulted with me, and I strongly approved. I contacted Menachem Begin, who responded to me with an invitation for Sadat to come, and he went.

It was a momentous event. The First Baptist Church in Washington, where I attended services, adjourned early so I could go home and watch Sadat's speech. It was a harsh speech, laying down the maximum demands of the Arab world. However, it was not important what he said; it was where he said it. Then—through me—he invited Menachem Begin to join him in Egyptian territory, which turned out to be a disaster. The two men were totally incompatible. They were only together about twenty minutes and stormed away from each other in a spirit of anger.

Later, I decided that the only way to break this deadlock was to invite both men to come to meet with me at Camp David. I handwrote long letters to both of them, and they both agreed. And they arrived there, and I talked to both men. Before that I had a deep psychoanalysis of each man presented to me—very thick books. I never let Jehan read the one about her husband. But they turned out to be quite accurate. After studying those books, I knew both men. Sadat thought about complicated matters in a broad strategic, bold, aggressive, global fashion. Begin was just the opposite. He thought about things in a more detailed way. How would they affect the people that had supported him? How would they affect his own interests inside Israel? When I deliberately put pressure on both men, Sadat would respond to escape my pressure by talking about broad generalities. Menachem Begin would become involved in minutia, particularly in semantics—wondering about what does this word mean, what does that word mean?

I brought them together; however, as had been the case with the visit in Egypt, they were incompatible. I tried for three days to get them to talk about the future. All they could talk about was the past. And so for the last ten days at Camp David, I never let them see each other. Begin sat in his cabin. Sadat sat in his cabin. They ate at different times, different places. I kept them very carefully apart, and I went back and forth between them. While I was with Menachem Begin, Sadat was resting. While I was with Anwar Sadat, Begin was resting. And we kept going and made some progress.

Within that interim period we went to the Civil War battlefield at Gettysburg one day, and I made them both agree not to talk about the Middle East or about anything that happened since 1865. I sat between the two men in the limousine. We got to Gettysburg, and Sadat, all of his generals, and all of the Israeli generals knew the battle details—I was really amazed. However, Menachem Begin did not know anything about the battle. We had Shelby Foote with us, an expert on the Civil War. And so Begin was a little embarrassing to me, not having learned about Gettysburg. But when we arrived at the point where Abraham Lincoln had made his address, Menachem Begin recited it word-for-word. A nice event—that I will never forget.

Then we went back to work, not very successfully at first. Assistants were negotiating. I was primarily by myself with those two men and those whom they designated. One day we made the mistake of letting Moshe Dayan go and speak to Sadat. Ezer Weizman, who was here last year, was a friend of Sadat, as you know. Moshe Dayan, who did not know Sadat well, outlined to him a harsh summary of Israel's demands and said, "We will not make any concessions!" I was in a meeting in my cabin with my secretary of state and defense secretary. And I was informed that Sadat had packed his bags and called for his helicopter to remove him from Camp David. I was distressed because Sadat had promised me he would not leave.

I was wearing blue jeans, and so I put on more formal clothes. I went over to the window, and I looked out over the mountain side and said a silent prayer. Then I went over and confronted Sadat. It was the only harsh confrontation we ever had. I told him that he had betrayed me and broken his promise to me—that if he left Camp David and left me and the Israelis there, the condemnation of the world would be on him. And eventually he decided to stay. He only made two demands of me and my negotiation role. One was that we have a comprehensive agreement on behalf of the Palestinians, which is there. I hope all of you will read what was agreed in Camp David. And secondly, that all Israeli troops, all Israeli citizens, had to leave Egyptian territory in the Sinai desert. Those were the only two. He said: "Anything else you negotiate, my good friend Jimmy"—as he always said—"I will accept it."

There was a general consensus at Camp David that Sadat trusted me too much and that Begin did not trust me enough. Sadat was the most forthcoming member of the Egyptian delegation. Begin was the most reluctant member of the Israeli delegation.

We had gotten to the eleventh day. We had a breakdown because Menachem Begin had taken an oath before God that he would never dismantle an Israeli settlement. And one of Sadat's unchangeable demands was that all Israelis had to be removed from the Sinai desert. There was one in Yamit, a little settlement, about 3,000 people in the Sinai desert. That was the fatal obstacle.

Begin had decided to leave. I had decided to leave, and so had Sadat. Begin asked me to sign a photograph of the three of us for his grandchildren. My secretary brought me eight photographs, and she had also discovered the names of Begin's grandchildren. So instead of just signing Jimmy Carter, I put "With Love to" and wrote the name of every one of his grandchildren. I took them over to his cabin. He was hardly speaking to me. I knocked at the door and went in. I handed him the photographs, a stack of them. He said, "Thank you, Mr. President," and turned around, dismissing me in effect. And he looked down and he read the first photograph, and he called out the name of his granddaughter. And then one by one he read out the names of his grandchildren. Tears ran down his cheeks, and when I saw them, I also cried. And he said, "Why don't we try one more time?"

I went back to my cabin with a man named Aharon Barak, who had been designated to be attorney general of Israel. He is now the chief justice of the Supreme Court. Barak and I worked out a proposal to submit to Begin, in effect saying, "You do not have to violate your oath. You do not have anything to do with dismantling your settlement. We will let the Israeli Knesset make the decision, yes or no. And you do not have any reason to vote." And to make a long story short, we concluded the agreement. And then later with about an 85 percent vote, the Knesset agreed to dismantle the settlement in Yamit. That was the high point.

After that things broke down again, and I could not get the Israelis to carry out the commitments that had been made. My interpretation—and Sadat's interpretation—was that Begin had agreed not to build any more settlements until the peace agreement was concluded. Begin, in my opinion (he disputed this), violated that commitment and said he only agreed to wait three months. So the settlements began to be built again. I decided to go to

Egypt and Israel in March of 1979. I called Sadat in advance, and he said, "Anything you propose, I will accept it." When I got to Israel, Begin was totally adamant against making any further concessions, and he and I had a terrible confrontation.

All the members of his cabinet, including Sharon, agreed with my proposal, but Prime Minister Begin did not. The last day I was to be there, Prime Minister Begin and his wife came up to my and Rosalynn's suite in the King David Hotel. We went down to the lobby to meet them. Our elevator got stuck six feet above the floor. It took them about twenty minutes with a big crow bar to tear open the door of the elevator. We did not know if God had His hands in the episode or not, but Begin finally agreed. I went back to the airport in Cairo, and we announced that a peace treaty had been concluded. We signed it a few days later.

Next spring it will have been twenty years. Not a single person has been killed. And not a single word of that peace treaty has been violated. And it has been a testament that it is possible for Arabs and Israelis who have despised each other and killed each other and have been at war with each other to indeed find peace so that it is permanently beneficial to both sides.

Then came another long empty period when nothing was done, frustrations grew, and violence erupted. Then there came a time of secret negotiations by the Norwegians. There was a social science group who went to Gaza to study the problems of Palestin-ians who were living in occupied territory in Gaza. They became trusted by the Palestinians, and as academics they reached out to the Israelis, too. First, a very low level of government increased upward. I was in Vienna, Austria, at a human rights conference in June of 1993, and Shimon Peres told me about the secret talks. He said the United States did not know about them. Later Chairman Arafat also told me about the talks. I was in the northern part of Yemen when I got a call that Arafat had flown into the capital and needed to see me urgently. I left my visit and flew down to the capital. With his eyes filled with tears, Arafat told me they had reached agreement and that the biggest problem for Rabin was to notify the secretary of state of the United States, whose government had not been involved. They rented a Lear jet in Geneva and flew to Los Angeles and informed Warren Christopher that the Oslo agreement had been signed.

There was a ceremony on the south lawn. Some of you were there. I was there, sitting in the front row and my wife in the third row. Behind her were former secretaries of state. And sitting beside her was the foreign secretary of Norway, who had negotiated the agreement. His name was never mentioned. Two years later he died at the age of forty-four. This signing was a high point. And then began the low points with Rabin's assassination and violence by the Palestinian militants, which resulted in Netanyahu's election.

And then the long dry spell was interrupted recently by President Clinton, who brought the leaders to the Wye Plantation. You know the result which has basically put back on track the peace process. It is not quite back where it was before Rabin's assassination, but there is hope. Anyone dealing with the Middle East has to be an optimist. I am. Jehan is. Sadat was. Many others. I am optimistic not as a naïve foolish person. But I am optimistic because I know the Israelis and the Lebanese and the Syrians and the Jordanians and the Palestinians and the Egyptians. I know that the Israeli mothers want peace. And the Palestinian mothers want peace. And the Lebanese and the Syrian and the Jordanian mothers want peace. The obstacles are the politicians. They do not have the courage to honor the demands and the prayers of the mothers. I made this same statement in a speech to the Knesset back in those days. I do not know what is going to happen in the future. I am inclined to be cautiously optimistic. Those of us in this room who have demonstrated an interest in the process need to be involved. However mighty, some with authority, some without authority. All of us have some degree of influence.

We need to support President Clinton in his efforts. I sent him a congratulatory letter the day before yesterday. We need to strengthen the Jewish community in this country who are deeply concerned about the security of the honored land. We need to be conversant with the suffering of the Palestinian people who have dreams. And we need to resurrect in times of doubt, the image of the greatest leader I have ever met. His name has been given to this lecture series: Anwar Sadat.

Afterword: A Dialogue with Jimmy Carter

C. D. Mote, Jr., President of the University of Maryland: Thank you very much, President Carter, for the inspiration and guidance you have given us all and for this opportunity to sense your personal history of this period that is so critical to all of us. It has really been a treat for us to hear you and also to be guided by you.

President Carter has graciously agreed to respond to questions submitted by a distinguished panel of participants at a conference held at College Park this past Friday and Saturday. The theme of the conference was Major Unilateral Concessions in International Bargaining: A Conference on the Occasion of the Twentieth Anniversary of the Camp David Accords. Professor Telhami, would you please relay the questions from the panel?

Professor Shibley Telhami, Anwar Sadat Chair for Peace and Development: The first question is from Professor Saad al-Din Ibrahim from the Ibn Khaldun Center for Development Studies in Cairo, Egypt.

Many Egyptian insiders to the Camp David negotiations in 1978 were led to believe that you, Mr. President, were going to enlist Saudi support for the Camp David Accords, but that this never materialized. What is the truth to this claim?

President Carter: Well, this in the past, I think, has been a secret that has not been known by anyone except me and then Crown Prince Fahd, now King Fahd. Before we went to Camp David, I met with Crown Prince Fahd. He encouraged me to go and said he wished every success. When I left Israel in the spring of 1979 and flew to the airport in Cairo and got President Sadat's final approval of the exact text of the treaty and got into Air Force One to fly back to the States, the first message I got was from Saudi Arabia. It said, "We are deeply pleased at the success you had and the peace treaty that we hope will bring an end to violence in our region."

The Saudis were quite close to me as president. When I had a problem with oil, when I had a problem later on with the Soviet invasion of Afghanistan Christmas week of 1979, they were there to help me. The grievous aftermath of the peace treaty though was that almost unanimously in the Arab world there was a condemnation of Sadat and a boycott of Egypt itself. Only three Arab leaders refrained from that condemnation: King Hassan of Morocco, President Nimeiry of Sudan, and Sultan Qabus of Oman. Everyone else publicly condemned the statement.

As is often the case in politics, there is a difference in public statements and the private assurances. I can let you know that I had private assurances of encouragement from the Saudis to proceed. But publicly they joined in with other Arab leaders who objected.

I cannot claim that we did not make some mistakes in the way Camp David was conducted. It was complicated enough for me. Some people have said, "Why didn't you invite King Hussein of Jordan?" King Hussein would not have come. "Why didn't you invite some Palestinians?" Had Palestinians been there officially, Begin would not have come. So we had to—I had to—make a judgment about how restrictive we should be. But to answer your question, I can assure you—and the documents are at the Carter Library in Atlanta—that we had strong support privately from the Saudis, even though they did join in with other Arab countries in condemning the peace agreement after it was reached.

Professor Telhami: The second question, Mr. President, is from Professor Asher Arian of the Haifa University in Israel.

Do you now think that your efforts at Camp David helped you or hurt you in the 1980 presidential campaign? What element in the negotiation are you now sorry you did not press harder to obtain?

President Carter: In March of 1977, before I had ever met Begin or Sadat, I made a speech in Massachusetts. And I called for a homeland for the Palestinian people, to end their long period of suffering. This was a statement that was quite controversial at the time. When we concluded the Camp David Accords, it had mixed reviews among Jewish leaders in the United States and also in Israel. When I visited Israel later, some of the people who had become top leaders there thought I betrayed Israel by my apparent affinity for the Palestinians. And one minister of defense, a very influential man, told me that I gave away the Sinai, which should be under the control of Israel, and I returned Egypt's oil wells, which should have been retained for Israel. So there were mixed feelings about that.

I might say that almost invariably in any sort of political issue, the ones who feel most intensely are the ones who tend to prevail. And the ones who are just in general for peace or in general for progress are quite often moderate in their beliefs. They are not willing to sacrifice to bring about what's nice. We see this quite often in our country, for instance, with gun control. The overwhelming majority of Americans feel that AK-47s ought not to be sold to people through a gun shop. But when a vote comes in the Congress, or in a city government, or a state legislature, the intensity of the National Rifle Association prevails, and the guns, the machine guns, are still being sold that way.

I am not being critical. I hate to avoid the question. In 1980, when I ran for reelection as president, I was the first Democrat since Franklin Roosevelt who did not get a majority vote among the American Jewish community. By then the glory of the peace treaty at Camp David had dissipated, and the threat of losing territory in the West Bank and Gaza, the threat of a possible independent Palestinian entity or government, was genuinely fearsome to many Israelis and to those who supported them over here. So I would say at the time we signed the peace treaty, there was an almost unanimous favorable response, but over a period of time it dissipated. I would say in general the incumbent government of Israel draws support in this country from the Jewish community. And I think that is the way it ought to be. And that is probably the way I would feel if I were Jewish and were concerned about Israel being in danger. I think that makes negotiations very difficult. It made it difficult for me. It made it very difficult for Presidents Reagan and Bush and now for President Clinton.

The genuine and I would say legitimate fear of Israelis is that their security may be frittered away because there is not much trust on either side as you well know. The Israelis do not trust the Palestinians. The Palestinians do not trust the Israelis. And there is evidence on both sides because Netanyahu cannot control settlers, some of whom will now be forced to leave territory that they believe in the depth of their hearts and souls is ordained to them by God Almighty. There could not be a more deep commitment in human beings' hearts. And there are Palestinians, members of the PLO, Hamas, who are deeply convinced that Sadat and Arafat have betrayed the cause of the Palestinians and that any peace agreement with the Israelis is counterproductive.

I over-answered the question. But the point is, I do not have any blame for anyone who has deep feelings, you might say, on all four sides: the Israelis pro and con peace, the Palestinians pro and con peace. You can make justifiable arguments in every case. I wrote a book about this. It is called *Blood of Abraham,* which is, I think, a very provocative title. We are all descendants of Abraham. Those of us who are Christians, those of us who are Jews, and those of us who are Arabs. And what I did was to go to Israel and talk to members of the Likud and also members of Labor. I went into the West Bank and Gaza and talked to Palestinians who were basically moderate and basically fervent. I went to Lebanon when the war was still on. Shells were bursting around the president's palace while I was talking to him. I went to Assad in Syria three or four times. I went to meet with the Jordanians and the Egyptians. And I wrote a book describing not my interpretations but what they felt about the Mideast peace process. It is an interesting book. If you study this subject you might want to take a look at it. But I understand, I believe, the complexities and the deep feelings and the justifiable fears that exist over there in the Holy Land. And so we should not feel an element of hatred or animosity toward someone who disagrees with us. That is the root and the cause of continuous strife: We cannot recognize that our enemies are human beings and they might have some justifiable reasons for disagreeing with us. So, I hope that in the future we can all be more moderate.

Professor Telhami: Thank you. Last question, Mr. President, from Carol Gordon. Over the past two days, we have been discussing the Camp David Accords and the effect of major unilateral concessions such as that made by President Sadat. The issue of trust or lack of trust and the question of how unilateral concessions help build trust has been emphasized. Can you compare the relationship between Begin and Sadat with that of Arafat and Netanyahu, especially regarding the level of trust and mistrust between them?

And if you may allow me, Mr. President, since this is the last question, to take the liberty of asking you to elaborate on a statement that is related to trust, both here and in your book, which was: "Sadat trusted me too much." What do you mean by that, Mr. President?

President Carter: Do I have my choice between those two questions?

Well, you know, professors could go on for days trying to analyze the differences between Netanyahu and Begin. And I am reluctant to be completely frank in my opinion. You know, the TV cameras go on. But I will say that Begin, I always thought, made the most courageous decisions at Camp David. He had the most to lose when he went back home. Because not only had he made an oath that he would not dismantle an Israeli settlement, but he had led the most militant element of the Jewish society when they were still under the domination of Great Britain and had even committed acts of violence, which is well-known. But he was a man of great courage. And I would guess that he had probably the highest intelligence of any man I have ever known. He was a semanticist. He dealt in the meaning of words. Very effectively, I might say. When I proposed in my handwritten notes, which are available for you to look at, that the Palestinians be granted autonomy, he said, "Insert full, full autonomy." So I wrote in "full" at Begin's request. Unfortunately, they were not given any authority or autonomy afterwards for a long time.

Prime Minister Netanyahu is constrained, I think, by his own deep beliefs and also by his alliance with elements in Israeli political society that are more reluctant than he is to make steps to implement the Oslo agreement. And I think that he at Wye Plantation had to make the most courageous decision. It did not require a lot of courage on the part of President Clinton to go there and to negotiate. Even a failure would not have been devastating. But it took a lot of courage, which I admire deeply, to make the concessions that Netanyahu has made.

I would say that Sadat was totally different from Chairman Arafat. Sadat was bold, authoritative, and self-confident, independent, strategic in his thoughts. Chairman Arafat is not blessed with those attributes of boldness and independence. He has to deal with and has dealt for decades with a very fragile organization of disparate points of view. His continuing as chairman is predicated on his balancing all those conflicting opinions in trying to reach compromises that will retain his authority. Sadat did not have to worry about that. Sadat was, I think, overly immune to the condemnation of those within the Arab world who disagreed with him. I used to argue with him about that. He was impervious to this, which may be one of the causes of his assassination. So I think you can see that the four men are quite different. And I am not trying to exalt any above the others, except I have already told you how I feel about Sadat. But I have great admiration for Chairman Arafat, with whom I have spent many hours, and who came to me as soon

as there was an opportunity and said to me, "I wish we had accepted all the terms of the Camp David Accords. We would have been much better off had we done it at the time."

The other part of your question, Sadat was as good a friend as I ever had personally. Rosalynn and Jehan are close friends. My children are friends with Sadat's children. My grandchildren are friends of Sadat's grandchildren. He came down to Plains to visit me in my little hometown, six hundred people, just a few months before he gave his life for peace. And when I went to Egypt, I went to his little hometown. And I walked through the streets and talked to some of his neighbors. There was an element of mutual trust and accommodation and rapport of a political and human nature that was possibly unprecedented between two leaders of nations.

When I got to Camp David, as I mentioned earlier, Sadat told me, "Mr. President, my good friend Jimmy," he always said, "anything that you propose, I will accept. Except I have two demands. I want a comprehensive agreement for the Palestinians that all the Israeli forces would be withdrawn from the West Bank and Gaza." All that is in the Camp David Accords. "And the other thing is, every Israeli has to leave Egyptian territory. If they want to come back later and live there with my approval I will arrange that, but they have to leave. And with those two exceptions it is OK."

And as I said earlier, Sadat was by far the most forthcoming member of the Egyptian delegation.

Some of his top assistants resigned in protest because they felt that Sadat was too forthcoming, that he trusted me too much. And as I said earlier, Prime Minister Begin, I felt, did not trust me enough. I do not say that in a critical fashion. But Ezer Weizman, Moshe Dayan, Aharon Barak, and other members of the Israeli delegation trusted me a lot more than did Prime Minister Begin.

So the feeling of trust was mutual, and I am glad that he trusted me too much.

3

HENRY KISSINGER

MAY 4, 2000

I met today with a European leader, and he asked me who I thought the greatest man was that I met in my diplomatic period. And I said it was Anwar Sadat. If I were to name the single most thrilling moment of my public career, it would be when I sat in a study in Aswan with President Sadat and we were talking about the shuttle diplomacy that was then going on. An aide brought in a note, and Sadat read it, and he had tears in his eyes. He came over to me, kissed me on both cheeks, and said, "They have just signed the disengagement agreement in Kilometer 101." The first direct negotiations between Israel and Egypt in twenty-plus years had taken place. And he said, "I will now take off my uniform, and I will never again wear it except on ceremonial occasions."

And, of course, it was on one of those ceremonial occasions that he was assassinated. I am quite frank to say that I did not understand Anwar Sadat when he first became president. Our intelligence reports described him as a weak man who had been put into that position because he could represent no conceivable threat as president. And everyone expected two or three other leaders of Egypt to overthrow him at any moment.

And Anwar Sadat made many threats, many statements, none of which, to my shame I must say, I took very seriously. Because it was absolutely axiomatic with us that there was no conceivable way that Egypt would dare to start a war. And in 1972, really it was 1973, I forget what the correct date is, President Sadat sent an emissary to America, General Ismail, who was a national security adviser at the time.

I met secretly with him in New York—and I have to be very careful what I say here—because several of my former staff members in the State Department are here. If you see people around you moving their lips, they are people who are used to having me say the things they wrote for me. So I met with General Ismail, and he read me a message from President Sadat that ended with, "If this discussion succeeds or shows progress, the president will invite you to Cairo."

I wrote a note to one of my associates sitting next to me, "Do you think it would be offensive if I asked him what the second prize is?"

I cleared the story with Mrs. Sadat. I had no expectation of anything happening with President

Sadat except, frankly, the usual rhetoric that we'd been hearing for many years. But once I met him, I knew what I was dealing with.

Before I met him, there were intervening events. But before I go back to these, I'd like to explain what I mean when I say that somebody is a great statesman. I've been a professor, and I've been in public life, and there is a huge difference between being a statesman and being an observer. As an observer, you can pick your subject. You can work on it for as long as you want. You are responsible, primarily, to your conscience in formulating your ideas. And you have the privilege of changing your mind.

A statesman does not have the same luxury. A statesman is always, in a way, at the mercy of events that he cannot fully control. His problems are imposed on him, and he's got to deal with many of them simultaneously. And he cannot change his mind. He is, above all, responsible for the consequences of his actions.

A statesman has to take his society from where it is to where it has never been. And that is a lonely task. I mention all of these qualities because I met no other leader—and I've known almost all the top leaders of the last fifty years—who exemplified them better than Anwar Sadat. And the Middle East is a region of extraordinary passions.

It is not an accident that three of the great religions and all of the monotheistic religions emerged from this barren territory of monochromatic colors. Especially since the greatest things that exist are all

man-made. There is no natural creation that would give man the same sense of perspective as do the slabs of those triangles placed against each other to evoke that mystical quality one can sit and stare at for hours—the pyramids. And they always look a little different.

President Sadat used to have a little house overlooking the pyramids in Giza. One could sit there with him for hours, and he wouldn't say very much. There, one sort of became at one with that sense of eternity that the combination of light, majesty, and simplicity imposes. Now, in the Middle East, it is also the case that totally different approaches and historical experiences were in conflict with each other.

On the one hand, there is a country like Egypt, with an almost eternal rhythm of its own. A vast territory, the population of Cairo is larger than all of Israel. Therefore, the rhythm of Egypt is inevitably different from the rhythm of Israel—and also from the rhythm of countries like Syria, that are more artificial creations.

When I encountered the Middle East, it was, in its acute form, the Middle East of the end of 1973. And for those of you who believe that our intelligence service is all-encompassing and so dangerous to mankind because it knows everything, please keep in mind that we were totally surprised by what happened next.

I had become secretary of state two weeks before. I didn't know that the State Department had an intelligence branch. I came in on a Sunday and read the intelligence reports, just to see what we had. And there were two reports. One, from a week before the war broke out, that there were Egyptian concentrations near the Suez Canal. And the other that there were Syrian concentrations on the Golan Heights.

Being an amateur and not yet a professional, I thought this was rather strange. So I asked the various services what it meant—since it means nothing that maneuvers were going on there. I said, "I want a report every two days." And I also asked the Israelis, about whom I didn't know then what I know now, that they were taking in each other's reports. I didn't have to ask them both because they were both reporting the same thing.

The Israelis were worried that if a real crisis got started, we would start a peace initiative, which they were very eager to see since all previous peace initiatives had failed. Anyway, the Israelis reported the same thing. And every two days I was told that these were just maneuvers.

Until finally on Saturday morning, the Secretary for Political Affairs, Joe Cisco—or maybe he was assistant secretary in those days—woke me up (I was in New York at the UN) and said, "There's a little trouble along the Suez Canal, and if you get on the phone right away, you're going to be able to get it quickly under control."

Well, I got on the phone right away, but I couldn't get it under control. Next there was a meeting in Washington, and the question was, "Who started this?" Everyone was convinced that the Israelis had started it because they were still of the mind-set that the Arabs could not start a conflict.

Then I finally said, "Listen. I'm of Jewish origin. The Israelis do not start wars on Yom Kippur when half of their army is in synagogue." It took us until the end of the day to put it all together, and out of all of this emerged the conflict. I received a message very early in the conflict from President Sadat saying that he wanted to negotiate eventually. And I sent him a message which said, in effect, "You can make war with Soviet arms, but you have to make peace with American diplomacy."

Thus, we exchanged messages during the war, even while the American airlift was replenishing Israeli supplies. Yet, Sadat never led a public assault on the United States. Quite the contrary. On the day the war ended, he invited me to Egypt. I spoke before about the rhythm of Egypt.

One also has to understand the rhythm of Israel. Here is a people that was marked for extermination and has had a millennium of holocaust and persecution. That is on the one side. On the other side is an Arab point of view, expressed once by an Arab leader as, "Why should we pay for crimes that were committed in a different continent on behalf of a religion that we do not profess?"

And it is extremely difficult to bridge this gap. The Israelis established a state between the Jordan River and the sea. That whole territory, no matter how big it looks on the map, is only 50 miles wide.

And in that territory there lived two different people—the Palestinians and the Israelis.

How to bring about peace and coexistence in such a confined area is an enormous challenge. For the Israelis, moreover, every centimeter of territory has symbolic significance. And they live with the fear of imminent catastrophe. For the Arab side, its setback may have been humiliating, but it could recover from it. For the Israelis, a wrong judgment may mean catastrophe.

For the Arab side, it is possible to make concessions that deal mostly with behavior and definitions of peaceful relations. For the Israelis, any territory given up is irrevocably gone. They cannot reclaim it, except by war. This creates a psychological imbalance.

I mention this only because, when I met President Sadat, it was only two weeks after a war in which we had been arming his enemy, and the Egyptian Third Army was still trapped as a result of postarmistice Israeli moves. Almost the first thing he said to me was, "This is a psychological problem; this is not a political problem. And you have to help me to bring about a change in psychology."

Now I have often asked myself—though I've never asked Jehan, maybe she'll tell me—what President Sadat thought precisely. I know what he said. He was surely trying to end the image of the pistol-brandishing Arab wearing local dress, threatening everybody. He wanted to make Arab leaders acceptable to Western public opinion. Now did he, right at the beginning, mean to use the weakened Egyptian army and Israeli psychological advantage as a tactic? Or did he mean to augur a fundamental change?

You couldn't be sure at the beginning. By the time Sadat died, however he had started out, there was no question that he had ushered a real transformation. And that started from the very beginning. With the Egyptian army trapped, the issue was whether one could open a supply line to it by getting the Israelis to withdraw across the only access route. Or should one leave matters there and negotiate a more fundamental arrangement?

I told President Sadat that it would be impossible to bring about two consecutive Israeli withdrawals in a short period of time and that his choice would be to leave his army there and to negotiate a disengagement agreement. To get immediate relief, one couldn't make the bigger move. At that point, Sadat didn't know anything about me. For all he knew, I was tricking him or, odd as it is for me to admit, that maybe I was incompetent and didn't know what I was doing. He certainly couldn't have known.

Finally he said, "Let's leave the Third Army there and negotiate the disengagement agreement." If I was wrong, he would be losing an army. That was the enormous strength of character and faith Sadat had. If I may mention another instance—at one point, the question was how many tanks could the Egyptians put across the Suez Canal after the Israelis withdrew thirty miles from the canal? How many tanks could the Egyptians put into this zone?

You must remember that, at that time, no Arab was talking to the Israelis. I was the one carrying the messages. And of course, that meant that both sides thought that, had they presented their own case, they would have done a lot better than I. So Golda Meir, who was then Israeli prime minister, said, "Thirty tanks." My attitude was that I would deliver any message once and that I would not comment on it.

So I delivered that much. And Jehan remembers, no doubt, General Gamasy, who was chief of the armed forces, and Foreign Minister Fahmy. When I delivered that message Gamasy burst into tears of rage. He said to Sadat, "Mr. President, the Egyptian army will never accept this. If you want to sign something like this, you go ahead, but the Egyptian army will never go along with this."

With Fahmy carrying on in a similar spirit, Sadat turned to me and said, "Let's go in the other room." We went to the other room. Sadat said to me, "Does she mean it?"—meaning Golda. I said, "No, she doesn't mean it. What you have to decide is how long you want to hang in there and how much it is worth to you to keep getting more tanks. And if you hang in there, my judgment is that you can probably get 300 in a few weeks."

Sadat said, "Let's go back to the others." He told Gamasy, "I have accepted 30. Henry will get me more and you will sign the agreement." I don't want to go through all the details, but I got more, and when we had about 100, Sadat said, "That's

enough." And then he said something very important. "Now you go back to Golda and tell her this, 'If I want to attack, I'm going to put 2,000 tanks across the Suez Canal in one night. But I don't want to attack. And therefore, I'll put no tanks across the Suez Canal.' You'll tell her I won't use that number. But she has to understand how sensitive it is. And if we can make progress in understanding each other on this level, we will make more and more and bigger and bigger agreements." And that was his great contribution.

The temptation of negotiators is always slicing-salami tactics—to start with an extreme position and then to keep slicing the salami and make a little concession at a time. The great specialist in this is President Assad of Syria—a master salami slicer. The trouble with it is that you don't know when you are finished, and both sides hang in there until they have totally exhausted themselves. The other way is the Sadat way. To state a great objective and not haggle over every detail. And to keep in mind that what you're trying to achieve is not to look good to your subordinates but to look good to history. In this manner, President Sadat changed the whole pattern of thinking about peace in the Middle East.

He was violently attacked by Arab nationalists, but he did more for Arab nationalists by changing the image of Arab leaders in America than they could possibly have done for themselves. I had the privilege of negotiating the first two agreements with him, and from there he went on to his historic trip to Israel.

Today, everyone takes that for granted. But I don't know any expert who, forty-eight hours before Sadat announced that trip, would have believed that any Arab leader would simply and unilaterally announce himself on a visit to Israel, lay a wreath at the Tomb of the Unknown Soldier, address the Israeli parliament, and make a breakthrough toward universal peace in the area.

This was a move of extraordinary strength and almost prophetic vision. That is why I call him the greatest man that I have met. Anwar Sadat was not a pacifist. He proved that he could fight for his convictions. He was anything but soft. He could be very, very tough.

He was also very eloquent but, if Jehan will forgive me, he was not necessarily a great conversationalist—except, I must say, with my wife who was very infatuated with him. But with me, I might well sit there for extended periods of brooding while he puffed on his pipe and went on reflecting.

He had an extraordinary psychological understanding of the various American leaders he met, and he met four presidents in six years. All totally different from each other, he handled each of them with extraordinary psychological skill.

But I want to go back to the original point. Sadat had the wisdom to understand that a fundamental change was necessary. He also represented a country with a deep intuition for eternity through a long history surpassing that of Arab states created after the Treaty of Versailles.

I never believed, for example, that when President Assad met President Clinton that any agreement could possibly occur at one meeting. Because where President Sadat felt that he could speak for all of Egypt, President Assad has to balance conflicting constituencies and has to bring them along step by step.

When I negotiated with President Assad, every time I came from Israel to Syria, I had to report at three different levels. First to the president, then a slightly truncated version for the generals, finally a more truncated version for the civilians. And he had to meld all of this together.

Where Sadat would usually settle in two or three days or not settle at all, Assad dragged my colleagues and me through thirty-five days of harrowing negotiations that ended only after we had broken them up, which is one reason I'm more optimistic about the present status of negotiations between Syria and Israel.

Though the spirit Sadat introduced is no longer there, the impetus he gave is still one of the major factors in the negotiations. The last time I saw President Sadat was on his last visit to the United States. He had just met his fourth American president in six years, and my impression was that he was a little exhausted by the different personalities he kept meeting. But very optimistic.

He did me the honor of inviting me to fly with him to New York from Washington. He had concluded his trip, and he said to me, "You know, next March the Sinai is coming back to us. It's going to be a big celebration. And since you and I started this, you should come to Egypt and celebrate with us."

Then he thought for a moment, and he said, "No, you're Jewish. It is very painful for the Israelis to give up this territory. And if they see you in Cairo celebrating with us, they'll be very hurt, and we mustn't do this to them. I have a better idea." He said, "Let the territory come back. And then, a month later, you and I alone will take a trip through the Sinai, and we'll go to the top of Mt. Sinai where I intend to build a synagogue, a mosque, and a church. And this will be a more meaningful celebration of the peace process than if you come to Cairo."

Two weeks later, Sadat was assassinated. Now I have told you these stories about my friend because, with many ups and downs, with many hesitations, there are now peace agreements between Jordan and Israel, Egypt and Israel. And I believe negotiations with Syria still have a chance of succeeding, and with the Palestinians.

Of course, we have to understand what we mean by success. I don't think the negotiations that are now likely to conclude will reflect exactly the spirit that I've been describing to you. It will be more practical, more based on balance of power considerations.

But if they can bring ten or twenty years of quiet, they can also create the conditions in which people in the region can learn to live together better and to see things in a different perspective. However this comes about, it would never have been possible without the huge contribution of President Sadat.

Every great achievement in history was somebody's dream before it became a reality. And one of the extraordinary things is that my dear friend Yitzhak Rabin, who started out as a soldier believing in victory rather than in peace, became imbued as the process continued on his side with what I've described as the Sadat spirit.

About two weeks before Rabin was assassinated, the Israeli foreign minister, who was in New York, told me that he had just talked to Rabin and had tried to convince him that he really should make some sort of concession. Then he said to Rabin, "But why am I talking to you? I'm preaching to the converted." And Rabin said "No, not to the converted. To the committed."

Which meant that he might have preferred a different outcome but that he had learned that peace and coexistence were the only hope for the region. On the one hand, it's a tragedy that the two great leaders who understood this best should have been assassinated by those so committed to the passions of the region that they could not raise their sights.

On the other hand, their sacrifice, however reluctant the other parties may be, has created the conditions in which there's really no road back. And it's therefore that I always think of both of these men with enormous affection. Statesmanship is a rough business, and one does not form many human ties. Most of the time, the attachments that are formed are really related to the positions.

But here were two men whom I'd be proud to call my friends and whose deaths for me were like deaths in the family. This is why I want to thank the university for permitting me to speak here in tribute to one of my friends. And to be introduced by Jehan, who, together with her husband, was part of our family, as ours was a part of their family. So it is a great honor for me to have been permitted to speak to you tonight and to pay tribute to a great man. Thank you very much.

Afterword: A Discussion with Henry Kissinger

Professor Telhami: The first question is from Professor Page Fortna of Columbia University. The Disengagement of Forces Agreement negotiated between Israel and Syria after the 1973 war has been remarkably successful at preventing war between these two countries. In your memoirs, you have said that you thought the risk of renewed war was high. At the time, what did you think were the most important aspects of an agreement to try to prevent the resumption of hostilities? And in retrospect, how do you think Israel and Syria have been able to avoid another full-scale war?

Dr. Kissinger: Well, in those days, when the agreement was signed, the Israeli army was within twenty miles of Damascus. And Egypt had succeeded in making it an agreement of disengagement along the Suez Canal. The danger was that, if Egypt alone seemed to benefit from the war, then Syria would be obligated to resume hostilities and would probably be backed by many of the Arab nations. And it would probably lose in such a conflict.

The danger of inflaming the whole area at the height of the oil embargo was very real. This was not just my judgment or my associates' judgment but a judgment of President Sadat and of the Saudi leaders. For this reason, I thought we had an obligation to all the parties to try to bring about a settlement or a disengagement agreement.

We'd spent thirty-five harrowing days because, when Syria and Israel negotiated with each other, there was nobody who made the sort of moves that I described Sadat as being willing to make. It was an exhausting process. And some of my former associates who went through it with me, like Roy Atherton, who was assistant secretary at the time, were actually younger than I, but they aged a lot through the process.

Now why was the agreement maintained? First of all, in fairness to Assad, the agreement was meticulously maintained by the Syrians, including provisions that were never written down and, being simply understandings, could have been easily abrogated by denying their existence.

Another reason, maybe the most important reason, is that the military balance is unfavorable to the Syrians. At any rate, they would have suffered huge losses by resuming hostilities. A further reason is the agreement itself. You have to concentrate forces in violation of the agreement, and that in turn may trigger an attack before you can launch it.

At any rate, the agreement has been maintained for nearly thirty years now—twenty-seven years—precisely and has made, I think, a significant contribution.

Professor Telhami: The next question is from Professor John Odell from the University of Southern California. You have great experience as an international negotiator. Could you select two examples, one of negotiations in which you did a better job, and one where you feel you did not do so well?

Dr. Kissinger: No, you will not get a satisfactory answer to the second part of that question. And those in the audience who worked with me don't have a microphone, so they can't correct me.

We had a certain pattern to the negotiations we conducted. First of all, contrary to what you read in the biographies on me, more of my associates were Foreign Service officers than, I believe, has been the case in most other administrations.

Before we went into a negotiation, we used to spend a lot of effort asking ourselves what we were trying to achieve. And I had a number of people—like Roy Atherton, Hal Saunders, and Joe Cisco—who would write long papers for me on what the real issues were. So we did not go blind into a negotiation. We had the desirable outcome in mind, and we spent a lot of time on it conceptually.

Most of the negotiations followed more or less of the same pattern because we also spent a lot of time trying to understand the point of view of the other side. In diplomacy, if you want to be serious, you should not aim for total victory. You have to

leave the other side an incentive to maintain the agreement. For if they do not believe that it is also to their benefit, since they are a sovereign state, they'll break the agreement.

Now, of course, in terms of the ultimate outcome, the least successful one was the Vietnam negotiation. On the one hand, bringing it off, even though it was never accepted by the protest movement, was a great tribute to Richard Nixon's fortitude. Withdrawing 550,000 troops without calamity and keeping a political structure in place in order not to break faith with the people to whom the previous administration had made assurances was an extremely difficult feat.

What we misjudged was that Congress would not let us maintain the agreement. It cut aid to Vietnam by 50 percent every year and eventually cut it off altogether. Had we understood this correctly, we still would have had to go the route we did. It was one thing for professors and journalists to say, "Why don't you just get out?" First of all, it would have been bad faith. But second, when you have 550,000 troops surrounded by one million enemies and one million allies who would immediately become enemies if you started backing out, how would you conduct that withdrawal?

It is important to keep in mind that the choices are not always so simple. And it was one of those cases where we won the battle of the negotiation, but we lost the war to our domestic opposition.

4

GEORGE MITCHELL

SPECIAL LECTURE OF THE SADAT CHAIR, JUNE 13, 2001

I've been asked to speak about my experiences in Northern Ireland and the Middle East. I begin by going back to the summer of 1787, when a small group of American colonists gathered in Philadelphia at a constitutional convention. They had lived under a British king. They did not ever want there to be an American king. In retrospect, we can see that they were brilliantly successful. We've had forty-three presidents and no kings.

The product of the convention was the American constitution. The part of it that we call the Bill of Rights, to me, is the most concise and eloquent statement ever written of the right of the individual to be free from oppression by government.

That's one side of the coin of liberty. The other is the need for everyone to have a fair chance to enjoy the blessings of liberty. To a man without a job, to a woman who can't get good care or education for her child, to the young people who lack the skills needed to compete in the world of technology— they don't think much about liberty or justice. They worry about coping day to day.

The same is true of people living in a society torn by violence. Without civil order, without physical security, freedom and individual liberty come to be seen as mere concepts, unrelated to the daily task of survival. So it was for many years in Northern Ireland. Violence and fear settled over that beautiful land like a heavy, unyielding fog. The conflict hurt the economy. Unemployment rose, with violence, in a deadly cycle of escalating misery.

Of course, those words also describe life for many in the Middle East today.

After a half century of discord and only occasional cooperation, the British and Irish governments concluded that if there was to be any hope of bringing the conflict to an end, they would have to cooperate in a sustained effort to lay the foundation for peace.

Despite much difficulty and over many setbacks, the governments persevered. After years of effort, they were able to get peace negotiations under way in June of 1996.

The prime ministers invited me to serve as chairman. I had been involved in Northern Ireland long enough to realize what a daunting task it was. In making my decision, I reflected on my own life.

My father was a janitor, the orphan son of Irish immigrants. My mother was an immigrant from

Lebanon who worked in a textile mill. They had no education. My mother could not read or write English. But because of their efforts, because many people gave me a helping hand along the way, and most importantly because of the openness of American society, I, their son, was able to become majority leader of the United States Senate.

So when I, who had been helped by so many, was asked to help others, I could not refuse. That the people I was asked to help are in the land of my father's heritage was just a coincidence. That I could help was what mattered.

The negotiations were the longest and most difficult I've ever been involved with. Often, no progress seemed possible. But somehow, we kept going.

There was an especially bleak and dangerous time in the Christmas season of 1997 and the early months of this year. There was a determined effort by men of violence on both sides to destroy the process.

In early December we had tried to get agreement on a statement of key issues to be resolved and on a process for resolving them. Despite intense effort, no agreement was possible. When we adjourned for the Christmas holiday, the prospects were bleak. If they couldn't agree on a definition of the key issues, I thought, how will they ever agree on solutions to those issues?

Two days after Christmas, a prominent loyalist was murdered in prison. That touched off a sharp increase in sectarian killings, as a vicious cycle of revenge took hold. The negotiations were moved to London in January and to Dublin in February in an effort to encourage progress. But the opposite occurred. The process was moving backward.

It was in mid-February, on a flight from Dublin back to the U.S., that I began to devise a plan to establish an early deadline for an end to the talks. I was convinced that the absence of such a deadline guaranteed failure. The existence of a deadline couldn't guarantee success—but it made it possible.

It took me a month to put the plan together and persuade all of the participants. By late March they were ready.

I recommended a final deadline of midnight, Thursday, April 9th. They all agreed. They wanted to reach an agreement. They recognized that there had to be a deadline to force a decision.

As we neared the deadline, there were nonstop negotiations. The prime ministers, Tony Blair and Bertie Ahern, came to Belfast and sowed true leadership. There wouldn't have been an agreement without their personal involvement.

Blair and Ahern didn't just supervise the negotiations. They conducted them. Word by word, line by line, they put together a compromise that attracted support from a broad spectrum of Northern Ireland's political parties.

It was a dangerous high-wire act. A single misstep meant disaster. But slowly and steadily, with great skill and assurance, they got safely across the divide. President Clinton made an important contribution, as well. He stayed up all night at the White House, telephoning several of the delegates at critical times in the final hours of negotiation. In a tight time frame, a powerful focus was brought to bear, and it produced the right result. But the very fact that getting an agreement took such extraordinary effort was a warning signal of the difficulties that would follow as the agreement was implemented.

Finally, in the late afternoon of April 10, 1988, Good Friday, an agreement was reached. It's important to recognize that the agreement does not, by itself, guarantee a durable peace, political stability, or reconciliation. It makes them possible. But there will have to be a lot of effort, in good faith, for a long time, to achieve these goals.

I believe the agreement will endure because it's fair and balanced. It requires the use of exclusively democratic and peaceful means to resolve differences, and it commits all of the parties to the total disarmament of the paramilitary organizations. It stresses the need for mutual respect and tolerance between communities. It's based on the principle that the future of Northern Ireland should be decided by the people of Northern Ireland. It includes constitutional change in Ireland and in the United Kingdom.

It creates new democratic institutions to provide self-governance in Northern Ireland and to encourage cooperation between north and south for their mutual benefit. It explicitly repudiates the use or threat of violence for any political purpose.

In the past few months, I've been asked often to compare Northern Ireland and the Middle East. I'll try to answer that question right now.

I begin with caution. Each human being is unique, as is each society. It follows logically, then, that no two conflicts are the same. Much as we would like it, there is no magic formula which, once discovered, can be used to end all conflicts.

Also, my role in Northern Ireland was more extensive, and took much longer, than my role in the Middle East. So most of my comments will necessarily relate to Northern Ireland.

But there are certain principles that I believe are universal.

First, I believe there's no such thing as a conflict that can't be ended. They're created and sustained by human beings. They can be ended by human beings. No matter how ancient the conflict, no matter how hateful, no matter how hurtful, peace can prevail.

When I arrived in Northern Ireland, I found, to my dismay, a widespread feeling of pessimism among the public and the political leaders. It's a small, well-informed society, where I quickly became well-known. Every day, people would stop me on the street, in the airport, in a restaurant. They always began with kind words, "Thank you, Senator." "God bless you." "We appreciate what you're trying to do." But they always ended in despair, "You're wasting your time." "This conflict can't be ended." "We've been killing each other for centuries, and we're doomed to go on killing each other forever."

As best I could, I worked to reverse such attitudes. This is the special responsibility of political leaders, from whom many in the public take their cue. Leaders must lead. And one way is to create an attitude of success, the belief that problems can be solved, that things can be better. Not in a foolish or unrealistic way, but in a way that creates hope and confidence among the people.

Unfortunately, the pessimism in the Middle East today mirrors that of Northern Ireland in 1995. Confidence in the peace process has been shattered. The culture of peace, so carefully nourished over the past decade, has been replaced by despair and resignation. Among the many challenges faced by the leaders in that region is to persuade their people that there is a realistic path to peace.

A second need is for a clear and determined policy not to yield to the men of violence. Over and over, they tried to destroy the peace process in Northern Ireland. At times they nearly succeeded.

In the process, they committed acts of appalling ignorance and hatred. Such acts must be totally condemned. But to succumb to the temptation to retaliate would give the criminals what they want: escalating sectarian violence and the end of the peace process. The way to respond is to swiftly bring those who committed these crimes to justice and go forward in peace.

That means there must be an endless supply of patience and perseverance. Sometimes the mountains seem so high and rivers so wide that it's hard to continue the journey. But no matter how bleak the outlook, the search for peace must go on.

Seeking an end to conflict is not for the timid or the tentative. It takes courage, perseverance, and steady nerves in the face of violence. These were the qualities of Anwar Sadat, a man who devoted his life—indeed gave his life—to the cause of peace. Sadat had the courage to take bold steps for peace, and he challenged others to rise with him.

Sadat also exemplified the third need, willingness to compromise. Peace and political stability cannot be achieved in sharply divided societies unless there is a genuine willingness to understand the other point of view and to enter into principled compromise. That is easy to say but very hard to do because it requires political leaders take risks for peace.

Most political leaders dislike risk taking of any kind. Most get to be leaders by minimizing risk. To ask them, in the most difficult and dangerous of circumstances, to be bold is asking much.

But it must be asked of them, and they must respond as Anwar Sadat responded if there is to be hope for peace. I know it can be done because I saw it firsthand in Northern Ireland. Men and women, some of whom had never before met, never before spoken, who had spent their entire lives in conflict came together in an agreement for peace. Admittedly, it was long and difficult. But it did happen. And if it happened there, it can happen elsewhere.

A fourth principle is to recognize that the implementation of agreements is as difficult, and as important, as reaching them. That should be self-evident. But often just getting an agreement is so difficult that the natural tendency is to celebrate, then turn to other matters. But as we are now seeing in Northern Ireland, in the Middle East, in the Balkans, getting it done is often harder than agreeing to do it.

Once again, patience and perseverance are necessary. It is especially important that we Americans not be distracted, or become complacent by the good feeling created by a highly publicized agreement.

The election results last week in Northern Ireland revealed an electorate divided and uncertain. The people and the political parties face daunting problems in continuing the peace process. Some analysts were already proclaiming the peace process dead. I disagree. Certainly there is cause for deep concern. But it is important to keep in mind that pro-agreement parties received more than two-thirds of the votes cast.

It will take extraordinary determination and commitment to get safely through all of their problems, especially in view of the electorate's doubts. But I believe it can be done and will be done. It would be an immense tragedy were the process to fail now. The British and Irish governments and the political leaders of Northern Ireland have come too far to let peace slip away.

In the Middle East, we must be heartened by the progress of the last few hours, modest as it is. The International Commission, which I chaired, recommended several steps to achieve an end to violence,

the rebuilding of confidence, and the resumption of negotiations. Working with the director of the U.S. Central Intelligence Agency, the parties are trying to establish a process by which those recommendations are implemented. We must all pray for their success.

The people of Northern Ireland and of the Middle East deserve better than the troubles they've had over the past several decades. Peace and political stability are not too much to ask for. They are the minimal needs for a decent and caring society.

There's a final point that to me is so important that it extends beyond open conflict. I recall clearly my first day in Northern Ireland, six years ago, I saw for the first time the huge wall which physically separates the communities in Belfast. Thirty feet high, topped in places with barbed wire, it is an ugly reminder of the intensity and duration of the conflict. Ironically, it's called the Peace Line.

On that first morning I met with Catholics on their side of the wall, in the afternoon with Protestants on their side. Their messages had not been coordinated, but they were the same. In Belfast, they told me, there is a high correlation between unemployment and violence. They said that where men and women have no opportunity, no hope, they are more likely to take the path of violence.

As I sat and listened to them, I thought that I could just as easily be in Chicago, or Calcutta, or Johannesburg, or in the Middle East. Despair is the fuel for instability and conflict everywhere. Hope is essential to peace and stability. Men and women everywhere need income to support their families, and they need the satisfaction of doing something worthwhile and meaningful with their lives.

The conflicts in Northern Ireland and the Middle East are obviously not exclusively or even primarily economic. They involve religion, national identity, and competing territorial claims. But if there is to be a fair and lasting resolution of these conflicts, economic growth must play a central role.

I conclude on a personal note.

I am not objective. I am deeply biased in favor of the people of Northern Ireland. Having spent six years among them, I've come to like and admire them. While they can be quarrelsome and too quick to take offense, they are also warm and generous, energetic, and productive.

They've made mistakes, but they're learning from them. They're learning that violence won't solve their problems, that unionists and nationalists have more in common than they have differences, that knowledge of their history is a good thing, but being chained to the past is not.

In all of these things there are lessons for the people of the Middle East, as well.

There will be many setbacks along the way, but I remain hopeful because I know that the people of Northern Ireland are sick of war. They're sick of so many funerals, especially those involving the small white coffins of children, prematurely laid into the rolling green fields of their beautiful countryside. They want peace, and I hope they can keep it.

I believe that the vast majority of the people in the Middle East also want peace, and I hope they can achieve it.

When the Good Friday agreement was reached, at about six o'clock on the evening of April 10, we had been in negotiations for nearly two years and continuously for the last two days and nights. We were elated and exhausted. In my parting comments I told the delegates that the agreement was, for me, the realization of a dream that had sustained me for three and a half years, the longest, most difficult years of my life. Now, I said, I have a new dream. It is this. I dream that I will return to Northern Ireland in a few years with my young son.

We will roam the country, taking in the sights and sounds of that lovely land. Then, on a rainy afternoon, we will drive to the capital and sit quietly in the visitor's gallery in the Northern Ireland assembly.

There we will watch and listen as the members debate the ordinary issues of life in a democratic society—education, healthcare, tourism, agriculture. There will be no talk of war, for the war will have been long over. There will be no talk of peace, for peace will be taken for granted. On that day, the day on which peace is taken for granted in Northern Ireland, I will be finally fulfilled.

Afterword: Questions from the Audience for George Mitchell

Question: Now that there's a cease-fire, attention, of course, is focused on the next stage—so called confidence-building measures—and your commission, or committee, as the administration is now calling it, has proposed a freeze on all construction at Israeli settlements on the West Bank. And I wondered if you are suggesting that in a practical sense, or if you have a disposition against settlements, that the Israelis have no right to be there? Indeed, does it apply to Jerusalem? After all, Israel is declaring, and Jews have been saying for 3,000 years, that Jerusalem is their capital, and this is provocative to lots of people, lots of Muslims, lots of Arabs. Could it be that Israel ought to give ground on Jerusalem? Where does it end? In other words, Israel's very existence is considered provocative by a lot of people.

Senator Mitchell: I do not have a prior disposition against settlements. With respect to the last part of your question, that argument could be made—has been and is being made—against any step taken by anybody in any peace process. Therefore I don't treat it seriously.

However, I do treat seriously the question regarding the settlements because it is a serious issue, an extremely controversial one, and a very difficult one for all concerned. First, let's be clear. The United States and Israel have a very strong and close relationship. I believe in that strong relationship. I served for fifteen years as a member of the United States Senate, and I supported that policy and continue to believe it to be the correct policy. However, even in the best of relationships there are differences of view. These are two democracies, sovereign states, and it is

unrealistic, indeed unhealthy, to expect that they will agree on every single issue. And one issue on which there has been consistent disagreement has been settlements. Every American administration, for more than a quarter century, has publicly opposed the policies and actions of the government of Israel with respect to settlements. And you are aware of the fact that we cited specific statements by prior presidents and administrations to that effect. We quoted President Reagan's statements of twenty years ago to the effect that the most important thing to build confidence was a freeze on settlements. Although circumstances have much changed since President Reagan made that statement, that principle remains valid.

Second, it is not a new policy for consideration by the government of Israel. Prime Minister Menachem Begin froze settlements during the Camp David process. Prime Minister Yitzhak Rabin froze settlements during his tenure in office. It has been widely debated within Israel, and there are strongly held views on both sides, as benefits a democratic society, a truly democratic society, where it is openly and vigorously debated. So we felt it was appropriate to make that recommendation.

Now the recommendation has also been mischaracterized by some who have criticized our report. It has been suggested, for example, that we establish a moral equivalence between settlement activity and what we describe in our report as terrorist actions. There is no such equivalence in our report. There are no words that would make that possible. Secondly, we propose a sequence of steps beginning, as the parties have now begun, with an immediate and unconditional cessation of violence. And a resumption of security cooperation, to be followed by a series of confidence-building measures, reciprocal by both sides, one of which is a freeze on settlements but others of which involve serious and difficult actions for both sides. And then a resumption of negotiations.

We also said, and made very clear, that although these actions should occur in sequence and that a cessation of violence must come first, there cannot be a sustained cessation of violence unless it is followed by other actions. That is simply stating what everyone in the Middle East knows. It is obvious. Everyone should understand that although these occur in sequence, they must all occur, because it is simply not realistic to expect that there will be a cessation of violence, a resumption of security cooperation, and then nothing else.

So there is going to be a difficult period within which the parties will now work, with the timely and I believe valuable assistance of the United States, presently in the form of George Tenet. They must work out the timing and sequence of reciprocal measures to rebuild the confidence that has been so badly shattered. We were quite clear in our report—the timing and sequence of those steps are absolutely critical, and they can be decided only by the parties themselves. That's what they are now in the process of doing, and we pray for their success.

It is not so much whether or not it is our recommendations or some other initiative that forms the basis for coming together. What is important is that they take the steps necessary because, as both leaders told me in my last meeting with them before we issued our report, "Life has become unbearable for the members of our society," as indeed it has for both. We said in our report, and I believe with all of my heart and soul, that death and destruction will not solve the problems of the Middle East.

There is only one path to peace and justice and security, and that is through negotiations. There are some Palestinians who express the view that Israel cannot exist and they must be driven into the sea. And there are some Israelis who hold the view that the Palestinians must be, in their delicate word, "transferred" to someplace else, that they have no right to be there. Both are dangerous fantasies. They will not happen. History and geography have made it clear that there is a shared destiny, and they will live side by side in conflict or in peace. We hope that our report will make a contribution, however small, to their choosing the path of peace.

Question: Thank you, Senator Mitchell, for coming here tonight and giving us your insight on the Middle East peace process. My question is related to the prior question, specifically regarding the Israeli settlements. At this time, I understand that you are stating that this is only one of the issues that is an obstacle to peace, but it has been seen even in the media that the Palestinian Authority states that the Israeli occupation for the past thirty-four years is the root cause of all the violence and the bloodshed and that they adhere to taking your recommendations as a total package whereas it appears from the Israelis' perspective that they want to pick and choose some of the recommendations that you made rather than taking them and implementing them as a total package. I just wanted your perspective on how greatly that is impeding the peace process by picking and choosing, cherry picking, if you want to call it, rather than just taking everything that you stated as a total recommendation.

Senator Mitchell: When our committee met for the first time in November of last year, we made several decisions on how we would proceed. One of them was that we would resist the invitation to comment on each day's events and to attempt to act as some kind of judges over the actions that people were engaging in. We've adhered to that. We determined that we would adhere to our mandate and we would try to be constructive. So I have not, during the six months of the process nor since we issued our report, offered commentary on the events that were occurring at the time. Our report speaks for itself.

We made certain recommendations. We believe they should be implemented. What is occurring now is a disagreement over the timing and sequence, and the full implementation of all the provisions of the recommendations. We made the recommendations that we think the parties should

act on but we stated explicitly in our report that their adoption and timing must be determined by the parties themselves. That's the process that's now underway, with facilitation by the United States, and I hope it is successful.

I think while there must be knowledge and a resonance of history, there must also be a willingness to look to the future. One of the things that I found in Northern Ireland was a very deep and intense knowledge of history and a reliance on that history to justify the policies of the present and, most importantly, to justify an unwillingness to take steps into the future. We must know the past, we must honor history, and we certainly can't forget the tragedies that have occurred. But we must also be prepared to look to the future, and I hope very much that's what happens now in the Middle East.

Question: Senator Mitchell, I'd like to follow up on your answer and ask about the immediate future and long-term future in terms of the political leadership on both sides. Given the fragility of Prime Minister Sharon's coalition government, do you think he can make the tough decisions and concessions that will be necessary to satisfy Palestinians, and do you think Yasir Arafat has the leadership to take less than 100 percent of what he wants? So would you give us a political judgment on that?

Senator Mitchell: I think that one of the reasons I was able to be helpful in Northern Ireland is that I myself was a politician. I think I had some understanding of the tensions that exist for political

HERO

DAITHI O'GLAISAIN

Wood
20 x 12 x 12 in.
First Prize Sculpture
Created for President Jimmy Carter on the occasion of the Sadat Lecture for Peace
October 1998

'HERO'
Created for presentation to
PRESIDENT JIMMY CARTER
on the occasion of
THE SADAT LECTURE FOR PEACE
THE UNIVERSITY OF MARYLAND
October 25, 1998

PEACE AND PRAYER

NATALIA BLANCH

Watercolor
12 x 14 in.
First Prize Painting
Created for President Jimmy Carter on the occasion of the Sadat Lecture for Peace
October 1998

INTERNAL DISCOVERY

SETH GILBERTSON

Marble
8 x 6 x 6 in.
First Prize Sculpture
Created for Henry Kissinger on the occasion of the Sadat Lecture for Peace
May 2000

In the Artist's Words:

"The essence of this work is internal beauty. This form was not created by my will, but simply suggested by the stone. I see humanness in this because each of us has our own internal radiance which is hidden beneath a rough exterior. . . . This inner form is the essence of peace."

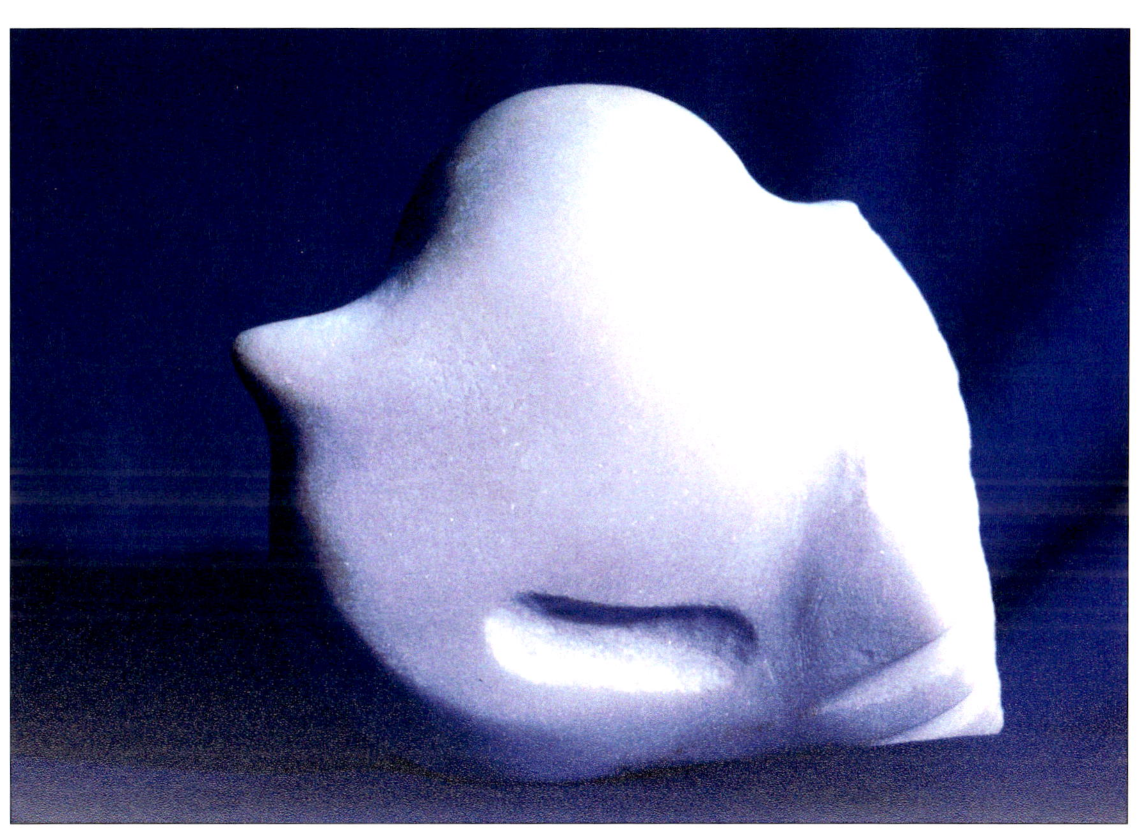

INTERWOVEN

LEILA DUNSMORE (1960–2007)

Lithograph
9 x 11 in.
First Prize Painting
Created for Henry Kissinger on the occasion of the Sadat Lecture for Peace
May 2000

SAKVOL KLIPPIETJIES (LITTLE BAG OF ROCKS)

DAVID PAGE

Limestone, steel, leather
6 x 4 x 4 in.
First Prize Sculpture
Created for Nelson Mandela on the occasion of the Sadat Lecture for Peace
November 2001

In the Artist's Words:

The student visited Robben Island—the infamous former prison off the coast of Cape Town, where the primary activity of prisoners was the quarrying of limestone. "It is not surprising that the lack of conflict is often mistaken for peace. The search for peace is futile because we are looking for the wrong thing. . . . Meaningful peace is simply a fortunate byproduct of a diligent quest for justice. The clichéd prison activity of breaking rocks can be seen in this work as a metaphor for steadfastness and resolve, facing nearly impossible odds. Once broken, rock cannot be reconstituted. Thus, this collection of fragments, tightly bound together, illustrates both transformation and unity. The forged steel loop represents the will of those who refused to see their position as inferior."

MEDIA AND ITS WORDS

VIRGINIA BLANCA ARRISUENO

Mixed media
17.5 x 22.5 in.
First Prize Painting
Created for Nelson Mandela on the occasion of the Sadat Lecture for Peace
November 2001

In the Artist's Words:

"Although the American media is beneficial and patriotic, I believe that the solution for peace is not only persuasion of the masses but also helping the American population better understand what is going on in the world. If every person, foreign and non-foreign, took the time to fully understand the situation nationally and internationally, the rate of violence would decrease significantly."

FIRST STONE

MARILEE SCHUMANN

Rice paper, stone
4 x 12 x 10 in.
First Prize Sculpture
Created for Kofi Annan on the occasion of the Sadat Lecture for Peace
November 2002

In the Artist's Words:

"The stone was perhaps the first weapon to be used by humans. Even now stones are thrown at soldiers and police in Northern Ireland and in Palestine. Stones are still thrown to punish and kill women in some countries. If the stone was the first weapon, let us bury the stone in layers of meaning and pages of words, in art and poetry, and in all the wrappings and trapping of human culture—until stones are no longer weapons but the subject and object of works of art, and until they become the material for building and rebuilding what has been destroyed."

OVERLAP

RUTH BOWLER

Mixed media
16 x 20 in.
First Prize Painting
Created for Kofi Annan on the occasion of the Sadat Lecture for Peace
November 2002

In the Artist's Words:

"When I think of peace, I am unconsciously drawn to a distinct space. I call this space 'Overlap.' It is the moment after we realize each other's differences and the moment before we decide what to do with them. In this fluid, negotiable space, the possibility of peace exists."

GETTING DARK

TAI HWA GOH

Paper, graphite
24 x 8.5 in.
First Prize Painting
Created for Mary Robinson on the occasion of the Sadat Lecture for Peace
March 2004

In the Artist's Words:

"The more devices are created and developed to make a peaceful world, the more unmerciful and destructive our world becomes. As more powerful shields are created, stronger spears and mutated monsters are born. . . . Every effort to make our world bright can also make the world darker. What can we do? Is the only thing we can do is to accept this darkness?"

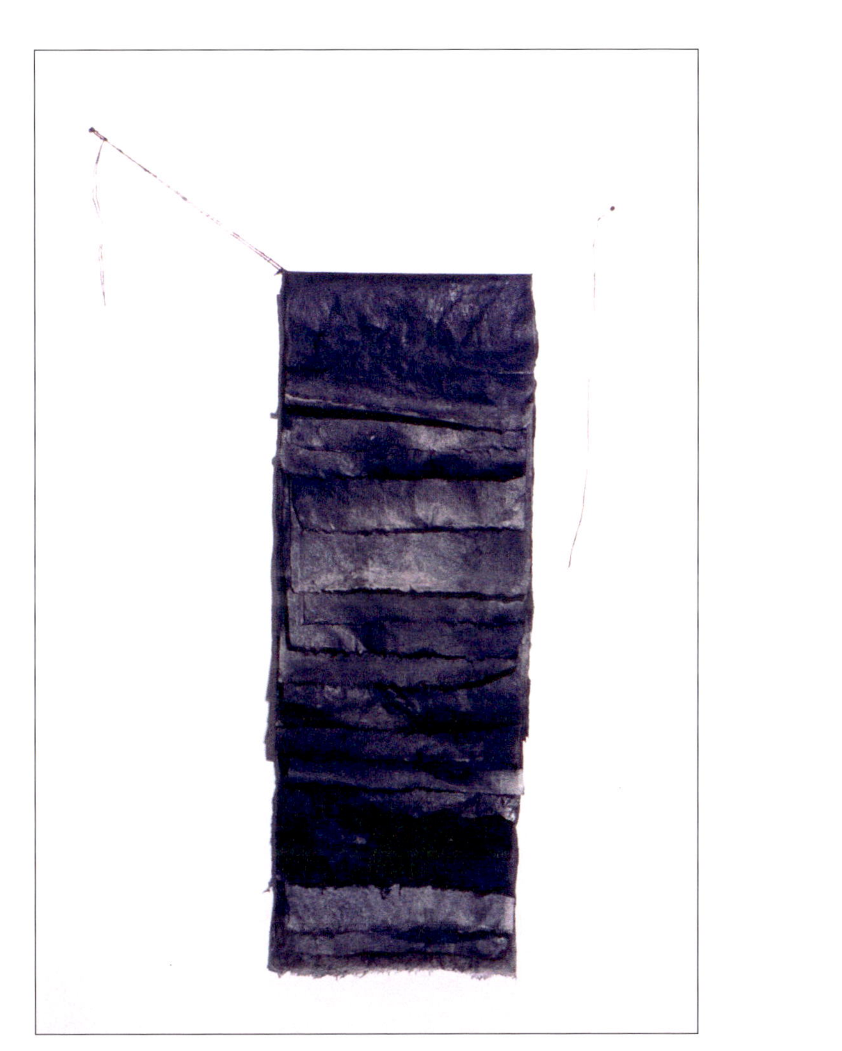

BATTLE RATTLES

CAL LEE

Cast metal, ribbon
8 x 6 x 2 in.
First Prize Sculpture
Created for Mary Robinson on the occasion of the Sadat Lecture for Peace
March 2004

In the Artist's Words:

"These rattles were conceived from my own experience with war and conflict—my grandfather's tales of serving in World War II; my father, who was deployed on his second tour of duty in Vietnam shortly after my birth; and my own deployment twenty-five years later to Bosnia-Herzegovina. I present these rattles not only to all the children who have lost a parent to war, or who wait for one to return home, but also to those who live daily with the terror of war and those who live in its remnants. While these rattles were born from and speak of conflict, let them speak more loudly of hope."

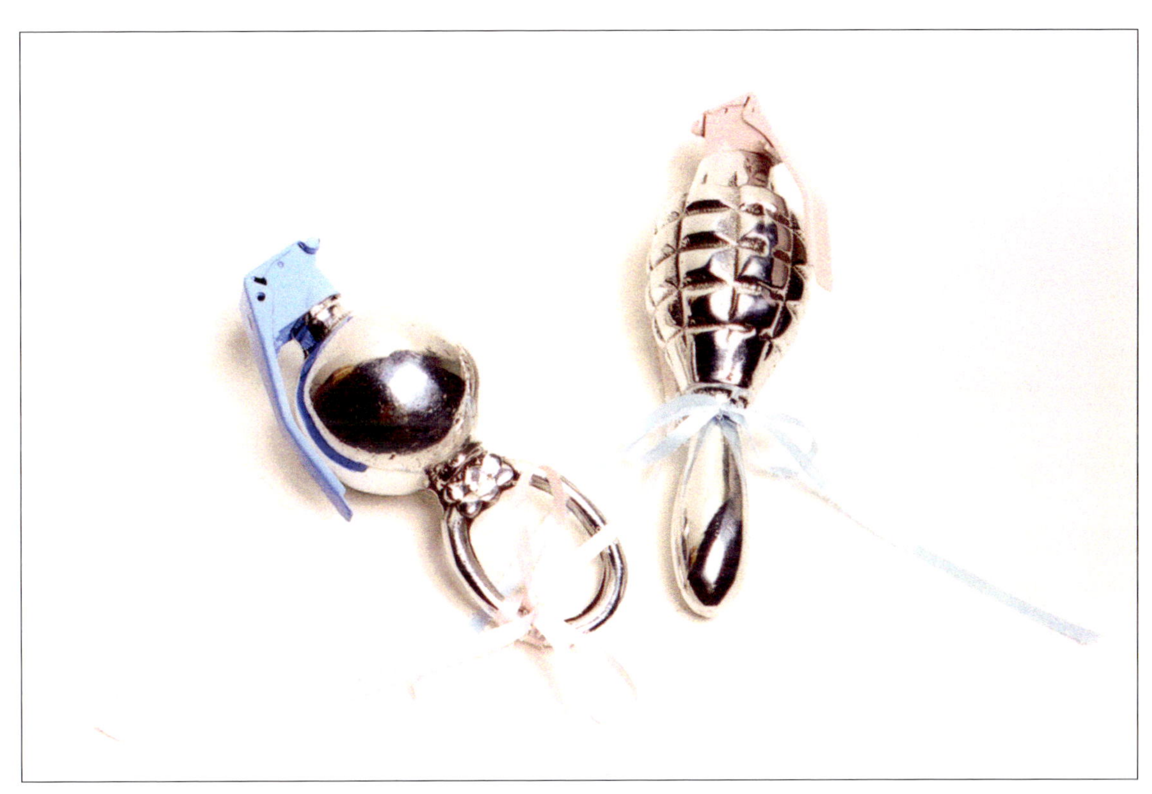

TECHNIQUES

BRIAN SYKES

Bronze, aluminum
6 x 12 x 6 in.
First Prize Sculpture
Created for James Baker on the occasion of the Sadat Lecture for Peace
April 2005

In the Artist's Words:

"The current multicultural world we live in is more like a bowl of chili than the ideal melting pot. Whether in my home of North Carolina, in the American South, in Southeast Asia, or in the Middle East, if individuals choose to stop working towards a discourse among dissimilar cultures, an understanding among them will never be reached. 'Techniques' is a piece of fused sculpture that … hopefully will remind viewers that memories are delicate, dangerous, and vitally important to constructing a common dialogue among a broad range of communities."

IRON HEART

JUDITH STONE

Iron
8 x 10 x 4 in.
First Prize Sculpture
Created for Mohammed ElBaradei on the occasion of the Sadat Lecture for Peace
October 2006

In the Artist's Words:

"This heart-form was made through a casting process using a 'reaction mold.' In a reaction mold, a form is built and imbedded into a mold that contains glass and other substances that 'react' when molten iron is poured in. In other words, the mold has baggage! Like the human heart, the molten iron seeks to fill the void of the form in the most perfect and complete manner possible, given the circumstances and issues [blatant or veiled] that must be negotiated. The outcome of a 'reaction mold' can never be predicted; awareness, history, and process blend into both tragedy and beauty."

THE OPPOSITE OF WAR ISN'T PEACE

KATHRYN CAPPILLINO

Mixed media collage
15.5 x 22 in.
First Prize Painting
Created for Mohammed ElBaradei on the occasion of the Sadat Lecture for Peace
October 2006

In the Artist's Words:

"War is death, destruction, and confusion, and this situation is the norm. However … despite war, disease, and destruction, we have the ability to create anew. That's what we need to do, create and renew."

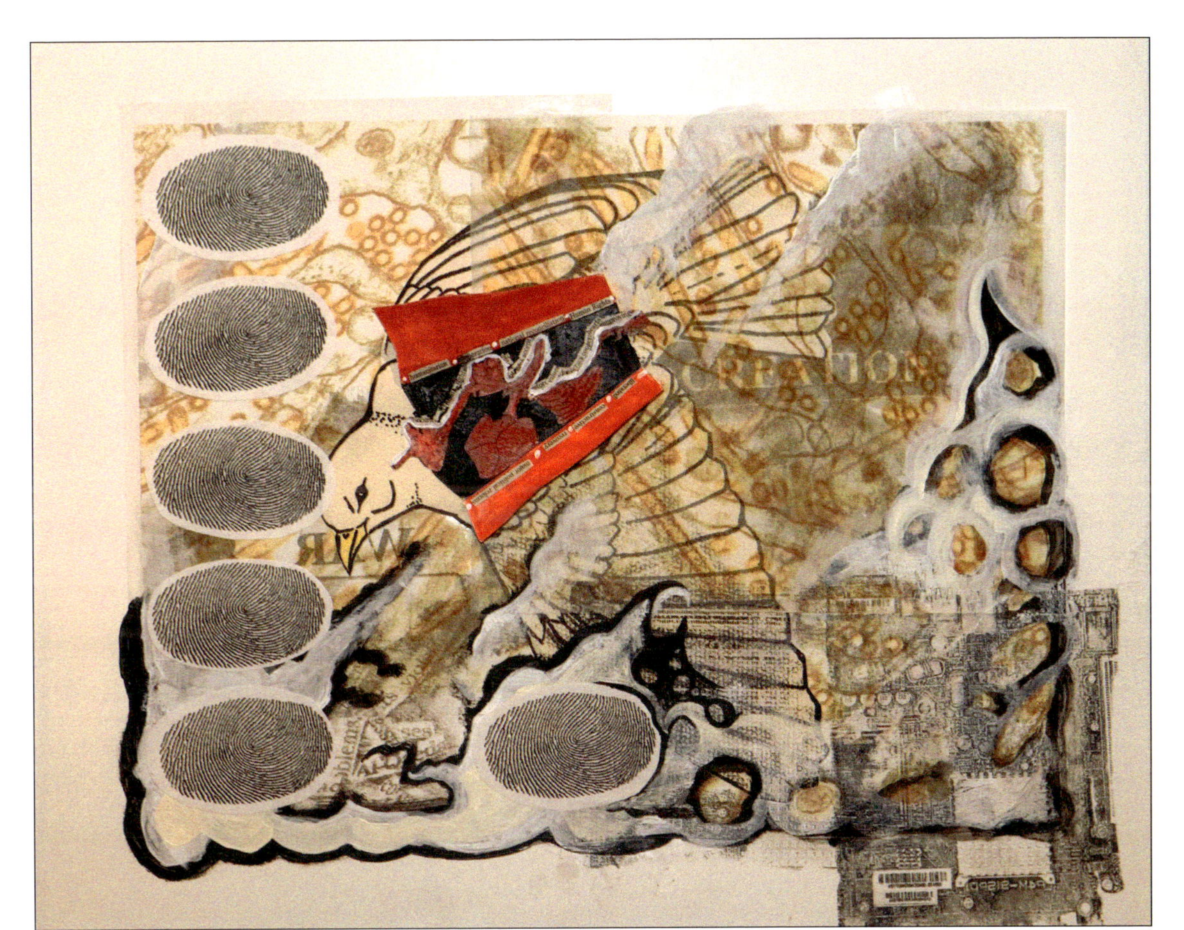

A FRAGILE POSITION

JEREMY FLICK

Acrylic, inkjet paint on plastic
6 x 6 in.
First Prize Painting
Created for the Sadat Art for Peace Program
March 2008

In the Artist's Words:

"My inspiration came from an excerpt of the Global Poverty Report (G8 Okinawa Summit, July, 2000). 'Poverty goes beyond lack of income. It encompasses economic, social, and governance dimensions. Economically, the poor are not only deprived of income and resources, but of opportunities. Markets and jobs are often difficult to access, because of low capabilities and geographical and social exclusion. Limited access to education affects the ability of the poor to get jobs and to obtain information that could improve the quality of their lives. Poor health due to inadequate nutrition, hygiene, and health services further limits the prospects for work and from realizing their mental and physical potential. This fragile position is exacerbated by insecurity. Living in marginal conditions with no resources to fall back on, shocks become hard or impossible to offset. The situation is made worse by the structure of societies and institutions that tend to exclude the poor from participating in decision-making over the direction of social and economic development.'"

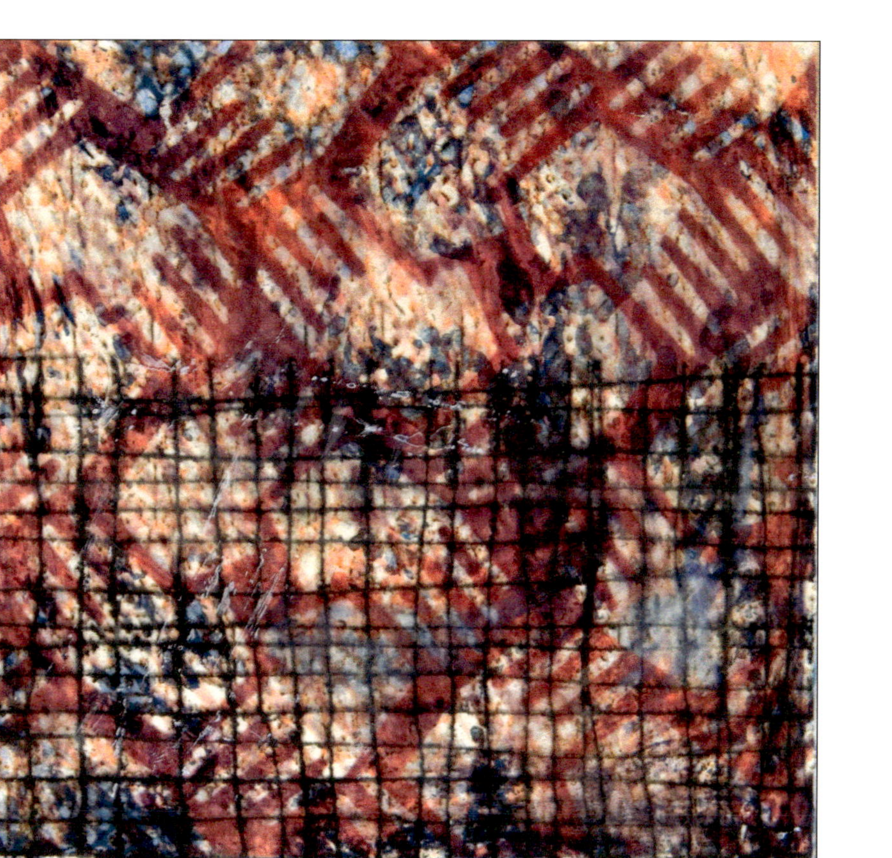

UNITY
SAMUEL MOORE

Bronze cast
11 x 5 x 6 in.
First Prize Sculpture
Created for the Sadat Art for Peace Program
2009

In the Artist's Words:

"This casting represents the difference in foreign policy that the United States will see over the next four years with its two distinct halves. The war on terror has proved to be a tough fight. While former President Bush did what he saw was best for the American people, the war has mostly bred insurgency and animosity towards the United States. Obama's foreign policy will revitalize relations in the Middle East, bringing a more orderly and joint effort to combat terror. The geometric base of this piece represents this solid joint effort. While the bottom of this piece represents order and unity, the top represents the freedom that comes from solidarity. The top needs the support of the base, just as the freedom that Obama wishes to provide will fall without a renewed relationship with our global partners. This piece is not strictly about the Middle East. It is a global piece, representing the same unity and freedom throughout the world. During the Bush era, America became a target of criticism by not only our enemies, but our allies as well. The Obama administration seeks to solve this and try to regain the good standing that America once had. It is only through joint cooperation that Obama will be able to support the freedom that the world desires."

INTERACTION
MALENA BARNHART

Latex, paint, soft gel, photographic transfers, India ink
48 x 22 in.
First Prize 2-D
Created for the Sadat Art for Peace Program
2009

In the Artist's Words:

"Foreign policy during the Obama administration seems to be moving away from the aggression and isolation that has stigmatized the United States during the last eight years. This piece is meant to evoke the magnitude of the task that the administration now approaches."

TRANSPARENCIES

AMANDA FOUST

Ink on mylar
30 x 76 in.
First Prize Painting
Created for James Baker III on the occasion of the Sadat Lecture for Peace
April 2005

In the Artist's Words:

"This work is about how the media focuses on a particular conflict to the exclusion of all others. . . . [But] there are always people fighting, people dying. The details become fuzzy, and few things stay in long-term memory. Someone reading the paper cannot remember who was massacred last month; someone reading my piece cannot remember what he or she read two lines ago. The facts are distorted, hazy, and half-remembered. Instead of peace in our lifetime, I think the most we can hope for is a lull, a moment of calm."

[illegible]

RELIEF

CAROLINE BATTLE

Aluminum
8 x 4 x 4 in.
First Prize Sculpture
Created for the Sadat Art for Peace Program
March 2008

In the Artist's Words:

"This work symbolizes the struggle with global poverty and the path towards solving it. The process of this aluminum casting involved burning and cutting, representing the pain and the poor quality of life so many have to endure in this world due to a lack of awareness and help. The forms resemble items such as bread or bars of previous metal, signifying the value of food and money for relieving the impoverished and sustaining a comfortable life. A bandage encompasses these forms, symbolizing the potential healing of the epidemic of global poverty through community and togetherness. It is through this type of group effort … that global poverty can be erased."

leaders who receive conflicting messages from their own constituents. At this very moment in Northern Ireland the political leaders are being told: we want you to settle this thing, we don't want to go back to war, but we want you to settle it on our terms. And "our terms" means one thing on one side of the Peace Line and something else on the other side. Of course the same tensions exist today in the Middle East, on both sides.

There is never a perfect time. There has never been, in all of history, a perfect leader. There have been great leaders. But men and women are required to take difficult action in less than ideal circumstances, and history has seen many examples of how people have risen to the challenge, have not been prisoners of their past, and have been able to take bold and courageous action to bring about the desired result, particularly in the pursuit of peace. Of course, we have discussed tonight one such leader in Anwar Sadat. Can the leaders in the Middle East do that now? I have no repository of knowledge or inside information to give you a definitive answer. I believe they can, and I hope they can. I believe that and hope that because the alternative is so unacceptable. We said in our report that this is a grinding, demoralizing, dehumanizing conflict. The most dangerous thing is that the public mistrusts each other, on both sides. People of goodwill in Israel, who thought they had a partner in the pursuit of peace throughout the Oslo process, now don't believe that they have. Palestinians of goodwill, who thought that they had partners who would accept the existence of an independent, contiguous, and viable Palestinian state on the West Bank of the Jordan, now don't believe that to be the case. There has been a corrosive loss of trust in both societies. That's what makes the task so very difficult. That's why it's so incumbent on us to say or to do all we can, each of us, in whatever way is open to us, to encourage the leaders to take the difficult steps to meet the challenges of peace.

Question: Senator, I'm an academic, but I won't make a speech. I will, however, ask you some analytic questions in comparing the two conflicts if you would. And there are four of them, and I'd like you to compare them in both. First, the weight of history. The Irish famine and the exodus to the United States and the long history of conflict with Britain on the one end. And, of course, for Israel the Holocaust, for the Palestinians al Naqba, the disaster, that's the first. The second is the issue of collection of arms, which seems in Northern Ireland now to be an extremely serious issue. The Israelis have demanded the collection of mortars and other weapons to make the peace process work. The third is terrorism. We saw in the case of Omagh in Northern Ireland that it almost but didn't derail the peace. And if you can compare the weight of terrorism on both sides. And finally, a bit more of a personal question, the role of outside mediation in both conflicts. If you could comment on these, please, comparing them.

Senator Mitchell: You may not have made a

speech in your question, but I will have to make one to answer it. The easiest answer is to the last part, the role of outside mediation or assistance. It is only possible if there is an acceptance by the parties themselves. No one, including the United States, can impose peace or a solution on anyone who is unwilling to accept peace. I think one of the reasons I was helpful in Northern Ireland was that in the first day of negotiations, the very first day, I said to the delegates that I am not here with an American peace plan. There is no Clinton plan; there is no Mitchell plan. Any agreement that emerges from these negotiations will be your agreement. Two years later, when there was an agreement, it fell to me to draft it, and when I handed it to them I repeated those words. Every word in it came from them. Admittedly, I had the important and subjective task of deciding what went in, and what didn't go in, and how it was shaped. But it was their agreement, and I think that was the proper role in the circumstances.

In the Middle East, it's slightly different. As you know, Mr. Tenet presented a plan to the parties for their approval. But if you look at it, it incorporates suggestions that they made. So I think a proper understanding of our role—an abundance of humility and restraint—is essential to success in that effort.

Now, as to the other parts of the question, I don't think I can or need to expand at great length. You have concisely summarized them. They are very, very difficult situations. What is most important is to have patience and perseverance in the face of setbacks. It is hard for me to describe to you the discouragement in Northern Ireland. For two years of negotiations, there was no progress. Think about that. I sat there for two years and listened to the same people make the same arguments. Nobody budged on anything. I was asked a lot by reporters, who do their jobs well, I mean no criticism of them, "If Prime Minister Sharon says no to this or Chairman Arafat says no to that, what can you do?" Well, if you took the position that if someone says no at any stage of the process that you simply pack up your bags and go home, there'd never be a successful negotiation. The whole reason that there is a negotiation and mediation is that there is a disagreement, and you have to patiently and with perseverance, and hopefully with some degree of tact and judgment, work to try to find common ground and to impress upon those participating in the negotiations the importance of reaching a peaceful resolution.

Question: Senator Mitchell, I'd like to ask you about how the international community has perceived this report. Recently you said during a trip to the Middle East that it was imperative that the United States exercise strong leadership moving forward. For those of us that have read the report carefully and covered foreign policy, it's become a bit of a Bible for how to move forward in the Middle East. And in a way some of us would argue that it's almost replaced U.S. calls for the parties to take steps. Now it simply asks them to implement the Mitchell report. I'd like to ask you if you were surprised how the international community has seized on your committee's recommendations in this way, and are you worried that if the violence continues, that the report and its recommendations will, that you'll be blamed for that—as a scapegoat in a way—and the careful recommendations that you made will not endure.

Senator Mitchell: On the latter point, that's really inconsequential. One of the other reasons I was able to be helpful in Northern Ireland was that I correctly perceived part of my role was to help deflect criticism away from the participants, who were active elected officials, and absorb some of it myself. So if, in the end, the process succeeds, I know all the members of the committee will be deeply gratified. If it fails and we are criticized, then it was worth the effort because the cause of peace is, I believe, so high and noble that it justifies the taking of risks, even though there may be some criticism. I think every person in this room would feel the same way. One of the things we did, at the invitation of the government of Israel and the Palestinian Authority, was to meet with the families of victims. It was indescribably moving. As you might expect, each side chose the most sympathetic victims to present to us. But it was impossible not to be moved by the sadness and sorrow and grief. So many lives unnecessarily lost, so many futures stunted, so much discord and upheaval that anyone who has the chance to be of assistance must do so.

I mentioned my parents earlier. My father had no education. He was a janitor at a college in my hometown. He was not a talkative man. We had very few of what you might call father-son talks, so those that we had I remember very well. When I was sixteen years old, I left home to go to college. My father said to me, "I know you're going to succeed," he said. "You're a smart young boy. I just want you to remember one thing. Every person has an obligation to help others in need. And the better off you are, the more successful you are, the greater the obligation." Then he poked his fingers in my chest and said, "Now don't you ever forget that." I have never forgotten that. So I think everyone has an obligation to help. Everyone, in whatever way that we can. The risk that there may be some criticism is inconsequential.

As to the reception of our report, it has been well-received. It has been endorsed by most of the governments in the world. Both the government of Israel and the Palestinian Authority have expressed general support for it. As noted in one of the questions, there have been some reservations on some of the particular points. So, yes, I must say all of us were pleasantly surprised at the reception. And having been exposed to the grief and sorrow and difficulty that has occurred and is occurring, we hope and pray that it will have some beneficial effect.

Question: Senator Mitchell, I thank you for your presentation and your eloquent speech. But I wondered if I could perhaps ask you a question that doesn't relate to the immediate political situation. I wanted to try and understand better how you are successful as a mediator, particularly when you have two parties that appear to be irreconcilably opposed. Do you seek to press each one to find what the limit of their flexibility and accommodation is and try to craft an accord based upon what is politically possible, or do you instead try to appeal to some kind of principle such as historical justification or self-rule and convince whichever parties necessary to conform to that principle of justice?

Senator Mitchell: I frankly hadn't thought of it precisely in those terms. But my immediate reaction is that it is some of both, depending on the circumstances. I had been a federal judge before I entered the Senate, so I'd had some experience in establishing a process by which there could be fair and informative debate, within a set of rules that provided some degree of fairness to the parties. Secondly, I'd served in the U.S. Senate. As I mentioned earlier, only half jokingly, the Senate has a rule of unlimited debate. As majority leader, I had to listen to most of it. I've heard sixteen-hour statements. One time a senator got up and said, "I want to make a comment," and he spoke for eight hours. I didn't realize it at the time but the Lord, in the mysterious manner in which He works, was preparing me for the Northern Ireland negotiations. So one of the principles I had was to simply apply the golden rule: treat everybody with respect and courtesy and give everybody the fullest opportunity to express their view. I said to the delegates on the first day, "We may never get an agreement, but not one of you will ever be able to say you

didn't have a chance to make your case. I don't even care how long it takes. I'll sit here and listen to whatever anyone has to say." Interestingly enough, privately both sides would come to me and say, "You've got to cut those guys off. They're going on too long." I told them all, "I'm not cutting anybody off." I sat there for—I don't know, I've never added it up—it must have been thousands of hours. I would listen for as long as anybody wanted to speak. If you really listen, over time there began to emerge common words, common themes, common ground.

If you probe, in a polite and respectful way, you can elicit from people an understanding of what it is that motivates them. Almost everything that we believe on first impression to be an irrational act, in the mind of the actor is not irrational at the time the act occurs. You must try very hard to get into their mind and understand what it is and not to have prior prejudice that says that's so awful, I'm not going to really listen to it. I think that is, if anything, the most useful advice I would give—patience and perseverance and understanding.

I go back to the point I made earlier—the aspirations of people everywhere are the same. They want to be treated with respect and dignity. They want to have hope and opportunity in their lives, and, most importantly, they want their children to have a good life. You've got to struggle and study and listen and work to find the ways to reach an understanding of all of them. That is what I try to do in those circumstances.

I referred earlier to the meetings with the victims' families. It was a painful experience, painful to listen to the grief and the sorrow of people who suffered unbearable grief in circumstances that are very difficult to understand. But you have to try to get inside their minds and you have to try, at the same time, to get into the mind of the person who committed the act. That is the manner in which I approached it. Try to figure out what it is and try to get them to agree to their common humanity and the universality of aspirations and hope.

[The next two questions were answered together.]

Question: Senator, speaking not as a member of the press or academia but as a member of the public, in my case as a Jewish American, last summer when Mr. Barak and Mr. Arafat were meeting with President Clinton in Camp David, their hopes were very, very high and very, very euphoric. And then something went terribly wrong. I have my own little theory of what went wrong, but I think you probably have a better one. My theory in a few words is the following: Oslo I believe is now seven, eight years old. I don't think Mr. Arafat did his homework during those years. He did not build an infrastructure for a Palestinian state as he was supposed to, so when it came time to sign on the dotted line, he got scared. And that worries me much more than whether or not next week, *Inshallah*, they will sign a peace agreement. Because what happens on the day after, if there is nothing to do after the parties have signed the paperwork? Senator, what is the answer?

Question: I don't think we could have had a better person than Senator Mitchell sent to the Middle East to negotiate on behalf of the United States. The United States has a great deal of experience in negotiations in very difficult situations in Vietnam, with the Soviet Union, and it's natural and logical that the United States will be a leader in the peace negotiations in the Middle East. However, as a psychologist I have a question that has bothered me for a long period of time. We have encouraged Israel and supported Israel in bringing to the Middle East 40,000 people that have been indoctrinated, trained, and practiced terrorism for forty to fifty years. They've also participated in arms smuggling, in drug smuggling, and many of them have American blood on their hands, like Abu Abbas, who was the commander on the Achille Lauro event, and Chairman Arafat himself, who directed personally the assassination of the people, the ambassador, and even Americans at the embassy in Sudan in the beginning of the 1970s. Is it realistic or was it realistic for us to expect the people that have practiced terrorism for so many years to come and be leaders for peace in the Middle East? They have caused a great deal of pain to the Palestinian people and to the whole region. The average income in 1993 for Palestinians was $7,000 per family. It's $1,500 now. And this is with all the assistance given by Europe and by the United States. I don't know how realistic it is to expect these people to really change completely, and maybe we should have thought about it much more carefully and should have encouraged the Palestinian people that live in the area to be negotiating on their behalf rather than a group of people that have been involved in crimes for many years. Second, just a very brief comment about the issue of the settlements. At the end of the war in 1948, there were 350,000 Arabs living in the area that was controlled under Israel. Their numbers have more than tripled by now. The number of towns and villages has more than doubled. Nobody has ever questioned whether they should or shouldn't have natural growth. Why shouldn't the same thing apply if, indeed, the Palestinians really want peace? Why shouldn't that apply to both sides? Why shouldn't Jews and Israelis be able to live in the West Bank just as Arabs are living within the state of Israel?

Senator Mitchell: Let me respond first over here. There has been some criticism of our report by those who hoped that we would conduct a review and analysis of the Camp David process and render a judgment on what happened there, with a specific condemnation following from that judgment. However, we were specifically instructed, in writing, by the president in our mandate to confine ourselves to the events that began in late September of last year. We were directed not to determine the guilt or innocence of any person or institution, nor to assign blame for any action. Therefore, the only response I can give to those who are disappointed in that part of the report is that it was specifically excluded from our mandate, and we honored the mandate. The question you raised is a very important one and will be answered by historians, by the participants, and perhaps by another committee of some kind. But it was not answered by this committee because we were expressly told we were not to answer it. I want to make clear that the parties agreed to the creation of this committee. The Sharm el-Sheikh statement, which called for the creation of this committee, was the product of a summit meeting which included the government of Israel, the Palestinian Authority, the United States, Egypt, Jordan, the United Nations, and the European Union. So, we did not answer the question because we were told not to answer the question, or any other question. Anyone who believes that our report fails to answer all possible questions about the Middle East is correct. It does not answer all questions, even one of as critical importance as that one, for the reason that I've stated, and I can offer no explanation beyond that.

Now, with respect to the question you have raised, it is of course a question that is raised in many contexts. When Nelson Mandela was released from prison, there were those who said he was a terrorist who could not lead people in any action other than terror. In Northern Ireland, I was asked that question almost every day. Could those who had engaged in violence in the past now be trusted to participate in a democratic government? And of course, as you must know, in Palestinian territories I heard precisely that argument made by Palestinians with reference to prior Israeli prime ministers. I do not know how to answer that question. Only time and history will tell.

But here is the reality. Palestinians have chosen a leadership. Whatever one may think of that leadership, it is their leadership with whom negotiations must occur. Otherwise there is simply no prospect of ever trying to reach some kind of negotiated settlement. I believe in a negotiated settlement. I want to emphasize the very strong part of our report that specifically, categorically, and strongly condemns the use of terrorism. It could not be more clear.

In Northern Ireland, when the negotiations began, they were based upon what became known as the Mitchell principles, which are principles of commitment to democracy and nonviolence. I believe strongly that in these circumstances, there can be no meaningful negotiation in an atmosphere of violence. I urge the condemnation of violence and support the use of exclusively democratic and peaceful means. But it is not for me, in my role, to judge who any group of people should select as their representatives. It falls upon me, in my role, to deal with those who are there by virtue of the fact that they are the chosen representatives of their people. Much as I might think otherwise, whatever my personal views or inclinations are, that's the reality that has to be dealt with.

As I said earlier, there's no perfect time, and there are no perfect leaders. Each and every person on this earth is a fallible human being who has made mistakes. I've made many mistakes, which I will not discuss with you now or at any other time. You have to deal with the situation that exists. And the situation that exists now is that there is an established leadership of the Palestinian Authority. It must be dealt with. I think the Israeli government recognizes and acknowledges that. What we have to do now is to go forward and find a way to peaceful, democratic dialogue to end the violence; rebuild confidence; resume negotiations; and reach peace, justice, and security for the people in that region. I believe it is possible, and I believe it will happen. And I hope very much that everyone here will do all they can to support that result. Thank you all very much.

5

NELSON MANDELA

NOVEMBER 14, 2001

It is a great honor to have been invited to deliver this lecture in the name of Anwar el-Sadat, a great African leader and man who in his life faced and dealt with the complex challenges of making peace, whether within a single nation or amongst nations. One can of course not speak of Anwar Sadat without thinking of and paying tribute to his great mentor and presidential predecessor, Colonel Gamal Abdel Nasser. His name shines brightly in the gallery of African heroes, liberators, and statesmen, and we salute his memory tonight.

Many of you will remember that in Africa, there were two blocs—the Monrovian group and the Casablanca group. The Casablanca group was the most progressive in its attitude toward the liberation movements in Africa and in relation to its attitude toward the Western world. And Egypt, under Colonel Nasser as well as King Mohammed V of Morocco, Algeria, Ghana, and Mali were in the Casablanca group, and it is in the light of this background that, in addition to Anwar Sadat, we think of Colonel Nasser.

It was thought proper to give as the title to our own autobiography the phrase *Long Walk To Freedom*.

I shall not pretend to be a literary critic even where it concerns a work written by myself. What I can say about that phrase is that it not only signals retrospectively the length of struggle to attain freedom and peace, it is also, one hopes, a call to readers to be ever attentive that the struggle for freedom and peace is a continuing one. We do not ever reach an end to a road where we can sit down and lay down tools.

Recent and current events in the world have forced us anew, and perhaps even in new ways, to focus on the complexities of maintaining, establishing, and consolidating peace in our own planet. We were hopeful that the beginning of the new century was increasingly witnessing the dawn of consensus about global responsibility for peace.

The terrible audacity of the events of September 11, 2001, shook all of us out of preconceptions about peace and security in the world. It is not clear that we have already fully comprehended the implications and consequences of what happened on that day, but surely the world will not be the same after those events.

The events, with such cold-blooded efficiency executed in the heart of the most powerful nation in the world, reminded us that the entire world stands exposed to terrorism that confounds because of its utter and ultimate lack of respect for law and convention.

Acts of terrorism have of course not been confined to those we saw in New York and Washington on September 11. Many parts of the world, too many parts in fact, continue to be haunted by this scourge that is terrorism. It assumes many forms and presents itself as in service of many causes. . . . Its defining feature is its ruthless and deliberate attack on innocent civilians.

It was the perversely spectacular nature of the events of September 11—not that other lives lost are less valued than those—that focused the world's mind anew on the threat of terrorism. It starkly confronted us with some of the ultimate implications of the ultimate lack of respect for law and convention.

We have had occasion to express ourselves publicly in support of the current military actions by the United States and Britain in pursuit of those they identified as the perpetrators of the acts of terror. We accept that the United States and Britain are bent on bringing to book the identified terrorists and that the unfortunate civilian casualties that arise are coincidental. We accept that they will and are taking all precautions possible within a war situation to minimize civilian casualties and suffering.

But before I proceed, there are certain hard facts we must accept about this attack on the 11th of September. The efficient manner in which it was executed shows that the preparations for this attack must have taken a long time indeed. I wouldn't be surprised if those preparations took more than two years. What is disturbing is that the West, with all its technology, its intelligence services, its enormous resources, was unable to have a clue of what was being prepared. And they only became aware when the attack was actually launched. That has serious implications, and challenges some of the platitudes which the West has repeatedly told us, that they are superior in intelligence to the developing world. And the fact that they had no clue whatsoever of such elaborate preparations has got serious implications.

The tragedy of war—and therefore one of the main reasons why we should redouble our collective efforts to create a world in which war shall have no place—is that inevitably innocent civilians and bystanders suffer and die. In the process of war, infrastructure, so vital to the lives of ordinary citizens, gets destroyed. This is undoubtedly happening again in the military activities conducted by the United States and Britain in Afghanistan.

Those in that country—already so devastated by war and conflict—who refuse to cooperate with the international forces against terrorism, have brought this war on the country and are the ones in the first place responsible for this further tragic suffering.

We must wish that the military action needed in pursuit of the objectives against terrorism will be concluded in the shortest time possible and that the world attention can turn to the other forms of action required to combat and eradicate terrorism, thereby creating a safer and more secure world for all.

We trust that the international community and agencies will be giving all the humanitarian assistance possible to the people of Afghanistan, now already in the conditions of war and also in the longer term, as that country needs to be reconstructed after so much war and suffering.

We must trust above all that in Afghanistan, and all over the world, democracy will be established and the interests and well-being of the people will be supreme.

We shall not be as arrogant to dictate that one particular form of democracy that we are used to and practice in our own country provides the answer to all situations.

There are countries without the popular institutions we know that provide for the social and economic needs of their citizens to a far greater extent than many of the popular democracies. What one is asking for is that government serves the people and that their interests be the priority in national life.

In a world where, as we are now witnessing, the pursuit of peace and the conduct of war sometimes coincide, it is absolutely necessary that our international and multilateral bodies become more effective as agencies for conflict management, resolution, and prevention and in the fight against terrorism. The manner in which virtually all of the nations of the world responded to condemn terrorism

provides the basis for multilateral action, with the United Nations particularly key in this regard.

The support that the United States and Britain have received from the international community for their stance and action against terrorism must surely in the future encourage them to lend their strongest support to making our world body an effective and potent agency for dealing with these international issues affecting peace and our common safety.

It is common knowledge that the First World War broke out in 1914 and ended four years later. Twenty-one years later, the Second World War broke out, and ended in 1945. It is now fifty-six years after the end of the Second World War. There has been no world war. Indeed, there have been many conflicts, civil and regional, but no world war. That is because we now have international bodies in which the majority of the states are members and that the most dominant of all these is the United Nations, whose charter provides that members must seek to resolve their problems through peaceful means, and therefore it is the duty of every country, big or small, to respect the United Nations. We condemn countries, no matter who they are, that avoid the United Nations and take action independently of the world body and violate the integrity of other countries, whatever the excuse is, because in that way they are introducing chaos in international affairs, unless they say we can avoid the United Nations, although we are members, and go and attack another country, but you have no right to do so. It is something that we have to condemn in the strongest terms. If you are a public figure, you don't hesitate to criticize any country, even those countries who happen to assist in the development of your country. We must thank them when they do good, but we must criticize and even condemn them when they deviate from the basic rules the international community has laid out to ensure that problems are settled peacefully through negotiations and through respect for the international structures that have been created.

It is often warned that the current conflict should not be dealt with in a manner that divides the Islamic and non-Islamic world. We have right at the outset, and also in our communications with President Bush two days ago, said that any campaign conducted should be against terrorism and not against Muslims or Arab nations and people.

When this attack occurred, I made a statement in South Africa, which was publicized very widely, in which I condemned in the strongest terms the attack on the 11th of September, and I called for the accurate identification of all the terrorists who were responsible, both as the masterminds and those who carried out these acts, and I said that they should be heavily punished. But at the same time, I said I hope this attack will not lead to the rise of an anti-Arab and anti-Muslim feeling because it is not the Arabs, it is not the Muslims, who are responsible for this attack. Those people who have launched the attack and cover themselves as people who are act-

ing in the interest of the Muslim religion are hypocrites because the Holy Prophet Muhammad made it clear that human relations must be based on respect for one another, and that problems should be solved through negotiations. We almost regard it as offensive to repeat that warning as if Islam is in any way implicated. Leaders in the Islamic world have expressed themselves as strongly as any against terrorism, and those acts of terror have been strongly condemned. Islamic countries form as important a bulwark against terrorism as any other bloc of countries in the international community.

I must also add that when I came out of prison and I went to the Middle East, went round the Arab world, I was shocked because the Arab countries had been presented as countries that had no respect for democracy, where there are no votes, where there are no parliaments. Indeed, I found that there were no votes, there was no parliament. We want all countries, including the Arab states, to introduce representative governments.

But the West must not bluff itself and think that when they talk of democratic government, they are superior to the Arab countries. There are certain respects in which the Arab countries—especially the Saudi Arabian kingdom, the United Arab Emirates, Brunei—have served their people in a way which you do not see in the West at all. Saudi Arabia, for example, has free education from the primary level right up to university and at university, the students are given an allowance of $400 a month. They have free health services. There are no taxes. Houses are so heavily subsidized that to get a house is next to nothing.

You don't find that in the West. You live at the center of New York, and you go to Harlem. You will find that poverty will stare you in the face. Of course, we find poverty everywhere, including the Arab countries. But from the point of view of treating their people, the Arabs are doing far better than the West. And talking about Saudi Arabia and UAE, the leader of government has more contact with his people than is done in the West. In Saudi Arabia, the crown prince, who is now the virtual ruler, every Tuesday, he sees anybody that wants to see him. He sees thousands, listens to their demands and their complaints, and wherever possible tries to address them. Nothing of the sort in the West.

And you must also realize that in a country like the United States of America, you cannot be a mayor, a governor, or a president if you are not wealthy. I was reading the other day to find that a mayoral campaign cost one candidate $300 million. Where would a common man get $300 million to be able to be a mayor, to be a governor, to be a president? So especially students, and all those of thought, must understand what is the world in which they live, and they must not be taken up by propaganda, which in many cases is actuated by other interests different from serving the nation.

The longer-term issues in the fight to eradicate terrorism—and this does not mean that these will have to wait for later to be addressed—concern the resolution of conflicts in many areas and the developmental needs of poorer countries and regions.

It is appropriate in this Sadat Lecture that we should point specifically to the situation in the Middle East and the imperative that a lasting and just settlement is found to that long simmering conflict. Toward the end of 1999, we visited a number of capitals in that region and stipulated three conditions for finding a settlement. We repeat those conditions now.

Firstly, the withdrawal of Israel from all occupied Arab territories.

Secondly, the unequivocal commitment by the Arab countries to the right of Israel to exist within secure borders. The aim of the attack by the Arab states on Israel in 1967 was to obliterate Israel from the face of the earth. Israel fought back and defeated the Arab army. So the Arabs must themselves make a clear statement that they recognize the existence of the state of Israel within secured boundaries and also to establish diplomatic relations with that country.

Thirdly, an international commission acceptable to both parties, to oversee the negotiations and implementation of these agreements. That is what will bring about a solution. The Western countries, ever since the end of the Six Day War in 1967, have been trying to bring about peace in the Middle East, not so much peace for the Middle East. The main aim of each country was to make sure that each country will have the honor of having brought about peace in the Middle East. As a result, there was competition. The United States of America and Britain would make a move. France would oppose that move. Russia would oppose France, Britain, and the United States. So there was that competition and that is why I suggested that we must have an international negotiating machinery composed of the United States, Britain, France, Saudi Arabia, and Egypt. And when I said this to President Bush the other day, after expressing my serious reservations that he refused to meet President Arafat when he had met Mr. Sharon, I said, "Mr. President, that was a serious mistake. That confirms the perception that the United States is a friend of Israel and therefore is not an impartial negotiator." And I said to him, "You must accept this proposal because it is the only one that will bring about peace in the Middle East." And I made it clear that I have never doubted the integrity of President Bush, the father of the present president. I never doubted the integrity of President Clinton. I said "I do not doubt your integrity, but this is the perception, and your failure to see Arafat strengthens that perception."

At the same time, I must indicate that President Bush to me appears to be keen to do the right thing. He appears to agree with the statement that was made by President Clinton when he paid a state visit to South Africa. He said, "We Americans have been asking the wrong question. We have been saying, 'What can we do for Africa?' That was a wrong question. The right question should have been 'What can we do with Africa?'" And I side with the president. That was a radical change in the foreign policy of the United States. And I complimented President Bush for having invited leaders like President Mbeki, President Obasanjo of Nigeria, and other African leaders, to listen to their views, their demands, and to try and shape the foreign policy of the United States in accordance with what the leaders are thinking.

There are many other parts of the world where violent conflicts continue to rage. In all of these, the world—through the world body and regional organizations—needs to be involved as the common concern of all of humanity.

In Burundi, for example, we have just managed with the assistance of the international community to reach a political agreement amongst the negotiating parties with a transitional government of national unity installed on November 1st. Now the support of the United Nations and the international community is required for peacekeeping activities and particularly for the development of that poor country.

Ultimately, the world must take common and global responsibility for social and economic development all over the globe. While the divide between the rich and the poor, with the latter vastly outnumbering the former, continues to grow, we allow fertile breeding ground for discontent and for extremism and terrorism. Our fight for peace is also, and importantly, a war against poverty and deprivation.

The challenges of finding peace are as complex now as they were in the times of Anwar Sadat. The events of recent and current times may just be the warning sound for us to take a global responsibility for addressing the expressions as well as the underlying causes of terrorism and other threats against peace.

The long walk to freedom, the constant struggle for peace, continues. It never was an easy road, and is certainly not so now. We have to reconnoiter many difficult twists and turns, and find answers to complex moral and practical questions. A global partnership on all aspects of the quest for peace makes that road considerably more negotiable.

I'm grateful that you've had patience. You must remember that I am an old man. It is my privilege to speak as long as I have the strength to do so. I thank you.

6

KOFI ANNAN

In just one week's time, we shall reach the twenty-fifth anniversary of Sadat's visit to Jerusalem in 1977.

Seldom has a political move deserved so richly to be called historic. It caught the imagination of the world. It transformed the political landscape of the Middle East. And it defined Anwar Sadat as a historical figure.

President Sadat showed courage, decisiveness, and extraordinary political insight when he did what until then had seemed unthinkable for any Arab leader: he went to Jerusalem and declared directly to the Israeli parliament and people that, "We welcome you among us with full security and safety."

His visit represented an extraordinary leap of faith and imagination. He understood that the Arabs could not recover the land that Israel had occupied unless, in return, they offered full and genuine peace.

And he had the intelligence and imagination to make a gesture that sparked a response in the hearts of the Israeli people.

As a result, he was able to convince them that they really could enjoy peace with Egypt if—but only if—they gave up their occupation of Egyptian land. As he said, "There is no peace that could be built on the occupation of the land of others."

And, thus, his gesture started a process leading to a peace treaty between the two countries based on normal relations and full Israeli withdrawal from Egyptian territory. In other words, land for peace.

Alas, Sadat's journey also led, or at least contributed, to his untimely death. He himself must have known the risk he was taking, and that is the measure of his courage. Like Yitzhak Rabin fourteen years later, he paid the price of peace with his own life.

Looking at the Middle East peace process today, I wish I could say that those two sacrifices had brought a just, lasting, and comprehensive peace to the Middle East, or at least that the leaders of today had shown a similar level of courage, vision, and statesmanship.

Sadly, I cannot. As we speak, Israelis and Palestinians are still locked in bitter conflict.

Nor is there yet peace between Israel and its northern neighbors. The truce on that front remains fragile and precarious.

An atmosphere of gloom and defeatism has descended on the region. There is the same utter suspicion and absolute lack of confidence between the two sides, of which Sadat spoke in the Knesset. How right he was to warn that in the absence of a just solution of the Palestinian problem, never will there be that durable and just peace upon which the entire world insists.

On both sides—Palestinian and Israeli—only those who believe their enemy can be defeated by force and violence show a grim confidence in the ultimate success of their chosen path. Yet on both sides, that confidence is surely misplaced.

No matter what price they are forced to pay, Israelis will not abandon the state they have built.

Nor indeed, I venture to affirm, would the United Nations ever allow one of its member states to be destroyed by external force. It was to prevent such things from happening that the United Nations was founded, and twelve years ago in Kuwait, it showed itself capable of rising to the challenge.

But it should also be clear by now that Palestinians will never reconcile themselves to the continued occupation and expropriation of their land, nor renounce their claim to statehood and national independence.

They are just as firmly attached to their land as Israelis are to theirs and just as strong in their national aspirations. They, too, have a right to their own state, supported by the United Nations and by public opinion worldwide.

The only way to settle this conflict remains the solution envisioned by the United Nations Security Council, and indeed by Anwar Sadat in that historic speech to the Knesset twenty-five years ago: two states, Israel and Palestine, living side by side within secure and recognized borders.

And while the precise location of those borders is to be negotiated between the parties, surely no one doubts that they must be based, as Sadat said, on ending the occupation of the Arab territories occupied in 1967.

In that very year of 1967, shortly after Israel occupied the remaining parts of mandatory Palestine, along with the Egyptian Sinai and Syrian Golan, the Security Council emphasized the inadmissibility of the acquisition of territory by war and affirmed that just and lasting peace in the Middle East must be based on Israeli withdrawal from territories occupied in the recent conflict, as well as the right of every State in the area to live in peace within secure and recognized boundaries free from threats or acts of force.

That is the principle of land for peace, and that resolution, number 242, has long been accepted by all parties as the basis of a peaceful settlement.

Such a settlement is envisaged in the Saudi peace initiative, endorsed by the Arab states at their summit last March—and it remains the preferred solution of both Israelis and Palestinians—and President Bush in his speech to the General Assembly also endorsed this solution.

On this point, all opinion polls concur.

The majority of Palestinians accept the continued existence of Israel and are ready to live alongside it in their own state.

And the majority of Israelis accept that peace requires the establishment of a Palestinian state in nearly all of the territory occupied in 1967.

What is missing, on each side, is trust in the other—and without that trust, the hope of peace becomes hard to sustain.

Israelis, bludgeoned by repeated terrorist attacks, which take a horrible toll of civilian life, have lost faith in the Palestinian will for peace.

They ask themselves if the partner they thought they had found in the Oslo Accords really exists. They wonder if the Palestinian intention is really, after all, to drive them into the sea. Their doubts are fed by the words as well as the deeds of Palestinian extremists and by the joy that sometimes erupts in the Palestinian streets after a particularly bloody terrorist outrage.

This leads to increasing public support for the draconian security measures that have pushed more than a million Palestinians below the poverty line, and the majority of Israelis who favor trading land for peace are reluctant, with no peace in sight, to confront the powerful minority who wish to keep the occupied land forever.

Yet, tragically, those same draconian measures combined with the continued and intensifying process of Israeli settlement in the occupied territory have the effect of pushing the prospect of peace and lasting security further and further away.

Palestinians, on their side, have lost faith in the Israeli will for peace. They point to the unacceptable policy of assassinations of militants—some of them carried out in densely populated areas and causing large-scale civilian casualties. They note that Israel piles precondition on precondition for a return to the negotiating table and destroys the governing institutions of the Palestinian Authority even while calling for their reform. Confined by roadblocks to their towns and villages, and much of the time by curfews in their homes, the Palestinians watch hilltop after hilltop covered by new Israeli buildings and valley after valley crisscrossed by roads reserved for Israeli settlers.

In some places, Palestinian farmers have even been shot dead by extremist settlers intent on robbing them of their olive harvest. As one Israeli journalist has put it, this sends a message that it's not a war on terror in the territories but a campaign to deepen the poverty and hunger of the Palestinian population, and so to drive them off their land.

There are Palestinians who have courageously raised their voices against the wicked and counterproductive tactics of terror and suicide bombing. But in the present atmosphere, they find it hard to make themselves heard.

Given the events of the past two years, it was perhaps inevitable that both peoples would come to doubt, fundamentally, each other's real commitment to peace. With every passing day, such doubts become more deeply embedded, and the task of renewing political negotiations gets even harder.

Somehow, we have to restore hope to both peoples by patiently rebuilding their trust in each other. And that is what the Quartet of interested external parties—the United Nations, United States, European Union, and Russian Federation—is seeking to do by setting out a credible road map, a road map of synchronized steps that can lead, within three years, from the grim situation we are in now, to the peaceful two-state solution that the majority on both sides desire.

This road map is being prepared with great care. It is now very nearly finalized. We in the Quartet fully realize that the credibility of this road map will depend on performance. But performance, in turn, depends on hope. Without a clear promise of the end result and visible political progress toward it, neither side is likely to summon the will to take the risks that each must take right from the start to improve the security and living conditions of the other. That is why we say that the process must be hope-driven as well as performance-driven.

And that, surely, is where all parties can learn from the example of Anwar Sadat. By all conventional wisdom, he should not have done what he did. Going to Jerusalem with no assurance in advance of any concessions from the other side seemed to almost all Arabs at the time an act of folly, if not outright treason.

Yet President Sadat understood the vital importance of psychology in war and peace.

He understood that political behavior is deeply influenced by the mental image that each side has of the other—and that sometimes this image can only be changed by an act of breathtakingly radical daring.

By a leap of imagination, Sadat understood that, while Arabs felt oppressed by Israel's seemingly overwhelming strength, Israel felt threatened by the uniform hostility of the surrounding Arab world.

More than anything, the Israeli people needed—and still need—the sense of being accepted by their neighbors in order to find the courage to renew negotiations in good faith, despite all the traumas of the last two years, and to make the necessary concessions.

In the stage the conflict has now reached, I believe both sides are aching for that sense of acceptance.

Many Palestinians, seeing the devastation Israel is able to inflict on their society, find it hard to imagine that Israelis also live in fear and that only by removing that fear can they hope to reach a new and more balanced relationship. Yet it is true.

And many Israelis believe they have already done enough to prove their willingness to accept Palestinians as neighbors and allow them space in which to develop their national life.

Unhappily, the life experience of many Palestinians has been very different, and Israel needs to do much more to win their trust. As long as the settlement building and land confiscation continue, as long as a political horizon is missing, as long as there is no real commitment to negotiate the remaining final status issues, Palestinians will never be convinced of Israel's desire for peace. That may be hard for Israelis to believe. Yet it is true.

The international community stands ready to help. Indeed, we must help both Israelis and Palestinians to break through the barrier of which Sadat spoke: "a barrier of suspicion; a barrier of rejection; a barrier of fear, of deception; a barrier of hallucination; a barrier of distorted interpretation of every event and statement." But we can only help those who are willing to be helped.

What is needed on both sides is true leadership, such as Anwar Sadat provided in his time. Let us pray that they find it before it is too late.

Thank you very much.

7

MARY ROBINSON

MARCH 17, 2004

It is humbling to give a lecture established in the memory of President Anwar Sadat, a leader who demonstrated that peace is possible, even in the most difficult of circumstances, if there is vision, courageous leadership, and bold action.

In this context of peace and conflict our thoughts go out to the victims of the bombing outrages a few short days ago in Ashdod, Israel, and those devastating bombs in Madrid just a week ago, aimed to kill and injure as many innocent civilians as possible. Yes, we were all on that train.

Language can be important in defining actions and in shaping reactions. I have always argued that terrorist bombings against civilian targets, no matter how appalling their scale, are not war but vile acts of criminality. Indeed, at a certain scale the perpetrators commit crimes against humanity under international law. The focus and determination of civilized nations to hunt down such criminals, their supply lines and money trails, should not be blurred by conferring on them the status of being at war. It has been disturbing to hear words like appeasement used to denigrate the democratic electoral process of the Spanish people, who have a long and stoic experience of combating terrorism.

Today is Saint Patrick's Day, and members of the Irish diaspora around the world—and our many friends here in the United States—are especially mindful of the complex, difficult, long-drawn-out steps in forging a peace process in Northern Ireland. The title I have chosen for my address is "The Journey to Peace: Finding Ourselves in the Other." It reflects what, for me, was President Sadat's great insight as a leader. He understood in reaching out to the people of Israel that he was reaching out not so much to a different nation or culture but to a shared human desire for acceptance, security, and dignity. It is, I believe, that ability to acknowledge the equal dignity and rights of each person which is most lacking in our world today.

Despite the advances in technology and communications that link us more closely than ever before, there remains the reality of division at so many levels in our world. We see these divides between rich and poor, between women and men, between different religions or ethnic groups, between citizens and migrants. We know as well that these divides are at the core of so many of today's conflicts.

In my experience, both as president of Ireland and as United Nations high commissioner for human rights, such divides were all too evident when I visited some of the globe's most catastrophic conflict zones. I listened to civilian victims, government leaders, and combatants alike in places both near to home like Northern Ireland and far away, such as Rwanda, Chechnya, Colombia, East Timor, Sierra Leone, the Democratic Republic of Congo, and Afghanistan.

A common thread in each situation was an unwillingness on both sides to see the other or the enemy as an individual with hopes and dreams and with equal rights. I saw how patterns of discrimination in a society drove wedges between communities. And all too often, I saw how corrupt and undemocratic governments fueled intolerance and denied people basic rights, thereby precipitating dissent and rebellion.

But you might ask, if the problems and their consequences are so clear, why does it continue to be so difficult to act differently and accept, as Maya Angelou put it in her wonderful poem, "Human Family," that, "We are more alike, my friends, than we are unalike"? I believe that getting at the answer requires, first of all, that we learn to deal more constructively with a very basic human emotion—fear. As we all know, fear comes in many forms. Fear of difference, fear that economic or social position is threatened, fear that identity could be lost in an increasingly globalized world—all bring about a range of reactions, and if pushed to extremes, to hatred, intolerance, and violence.

You can find signs of contemporary individual and group fear just by looking at public perceptions of current issues. Last year, for example, the Pew Research Center for the People & the Press published a survey conducted in forty-four countries which revealed that, although people generally have a favorable view of increased economic connections commonly associated with globalization, sizeable majorities of those polled believed their traditional ways of life were being threatened and they agreed with the statement that "our way of life needs to be protected against foreign influence."

A similar finding can be seen in an EU poll released just last week which found that while the majority of Europeans agreed that there was an economic need for more immigrants, 80 percent still want a tightening of passport and other entry controls for foreigners as part of a European Union asylum and immigration policy. Clearly, fear is one of the drivers of such seemingly contradictory views. And unfortunately in Europe today there are politicians and political parties only too willing to exploit those fears.

If fear is a main factor, education and factual information provide a remedy. For example, how many people have really considered the demographic realities that developed economies are currently facing? Aging populations and changes in the workforce make it imperative that industrialized economies increase immigration if they are to sustain themselves.

Moreover, how many realize that money sent home by migrants to their families in the form of remittances is a growing source of income that is vital to many countries? The International Monetary Fund reported that in 2002 alone remittances from migrants were around $100 billion, as compared with only $51 billion in global development assistance. How many more people would be forced to leave their homes if not for the remittances coming from their family members abroad?

As avenues for legal migration become more and more limited, would-be migrants have increasingly resorted to illegal entry and unauthorized stay. This has fueled the activities of human smugglers and traffickers who show little respect for the humanity of their cargo. Unknown numbers have died in transit, and those who do reach their destination often find themselves trapped in a cycle of abuse and exploitation—giving a new face to slavery in the modern era. They are part of a growing population of undocumented immigrants who find themselves vulnerable to exploitation in employment, to racist crime, and to security measures in the context of the ongoing war on terrorism. Can any of us say that we truly identify with the situations faced by millions of today's migrants?

The public debate in most countries around migration has thus far been marked by negativity, hostility, and fear of migrants. What is needed today is a new approach, anchored in human rights, that acknowledges both the potential problems and benefits for receiving and sending countries.

At the international level, a Global Commission on International Migration has been established to study these issues further and make policy recommendations to UN Secretary-General Kofi Annan in 2005. I am pleased to be a member of this commission, which must seek to reframe in a more positive way the migration debate, to understand that the rights of people who have left their countries in search of greater human security must be protected and that governments—both sending and receiving—must be accountable. Last month, at the commission's first meeting in Stockholm, commission members agreed that political leadership on this issue is vital.

In a speech at the White House last January to announce new proposals on U.S. immigration policy, President Bush set out some of the problems that need to be addressed. The president noted:

> As a nation that values immigration, and depends on immigration, we should have immigration laws that work and make us proud. Yet today we do not. Instead, we see many employers turning to the illegal labor market. We see millions of hard-working men and women condemned to fear and insecurity in a massive, undocumented economy.

President Bush went on to say that the challenge was to make U.S. immigration laws "more rational, and more humane." I recognize the importance of focusing on working closely with Mexico as it is the source of at least three-fifths of the United States' undocumented immigrant population. At the same time, I would point out the need to reflect seriously on policies concerning those from other neighboring countries who seek refuge and economic opportunity in the United States. The present situation in Haiti comes to mind.

Present U.S. policy toward those seeking to flee Haiti risks violating obligations under international law. According to reports from U.S.-based groups, such as Human Rights First, Haitians currently interdicted at sea are not informed of their right to seek asylum and are not interviewed by any U.S. official to determine whether or not they are in danger of persecution if returned.

As difficult as a new inflow of refugees would be to manage, we should call on the government to recognize that no migrants should be returned to Haiti if the situation there is so dangerous that their safety cannot be assured.

Important as the current focus on migration is, it should not cause us to neglect other forms of discrimination and intolerance which persist in the world today. One of the most disturbing of these is anti-Semitism. Much recent media coverage of anti-Semitism has centered on the situation in Europe, where synagogues and Jewish cemeteries have been defaced and Jews have been physically attacked on the streets. While many in Europe will point out that the situation is a complex one that cannot be easily equated with historical anti-Semitism on the

continent, it is vital that Europeans take effective action to stop these reprehensible acts.

Nor should we forget the anti-Semitic diatribes so common in the Middle East. Even in the United States on some prestigious college campuses, there have been attempts to cast Israel as a pariah state and equate its actions with those of South African apartheid, a first step toward questioning Israel's right to exist.

Allow me to reflect briefly on an experience during my term as high commissioner when I came face to face with such anti-Semitism. It was in a setting I had hoped would be one of tolerance and respect— the Durban World Conference against Racism.

I should give some brief background on the conference for those of you who may not be familiar with this event, which took place the first week of September 2001, just days before the terrible attacks on the U.S. on 9/11. The decision to hold this conference, the third UN global forum to address the subject of racism, was taken by the General Assembly in 1997. It was decided that the conference should address in a comprehensive manner all forms of racism, racial discrimination, xenophobia, and related contemporary forms of intolerance; that it should be action-oriented and focus on practical measures to eradicate racism, including measures of prevention, education, protection, and the provision of effective remedies for victims.

I should also explain my own role. At its session in 1998, the UN Commission on Human Rights requested the UN secretary-general to designate the high commissioner for human rights as secretary-general of the world conference. It is common for a secretary-general of a UN conference to be a senior UN official who is mandated with the main responsibility for the preparations and secretariat functions of the conference.

The decision to hold this conference in Durban, South Africa, was fitting, given the country's own legacy of racism and its inspiring example of reconciliation. As secretary-general of the conference, I was determined to play a role in helping make it a global event which would encourage each society to ask itself hard questions. Is it sufficiently inclusive? Is it nondiscriminatory? Are its norms of behavior based on the principles enshrined in the Universal Declaration of Human Rights? How best could the conference confront the many horrors of racism—from slavery to the Holocaust, from apartheid to ethnic cleansing—and agree on comprehensive measures to prevent them from happening again? To encourage positive thinking, I had earlier presented a vision statement of positive commitments under the patronage of Nelson Mandela, which more than eighty heads of state signed and which I hoped might influence government debates.

Unfortunately, some participants, both inside and outside the conference, wanted to make the conflict in the Middle East, which at the time had entered a new phase of violence, the principal focus of Durban. At the Non-Governmental Forum, a parallel meeting, which, as is common practice at UN conferences, was also held in Durban to coincide with the intergovernmental discussions, some participants resorted to blatant anti-Semitic speech and activities to convey their message.

And so, at a conference in which we were supposed to be defending human rights values, we found ourselves faced with appalling bigotry and intolerance. I and many others condemned such language and, in the circumstances, I refused to recommend the final NGO document to the conference.

Meanwhile in the conference itself, which was, of course, intergovernmental, attempts were also being made to insert unacceptable language concerning Israel which had first emerged—in brackets, and therefore not as agreed text—at the Asia regional preparatory meeting for the conference, which was held in Tehran in February 2001. I should point out here that, as is the practice in UN conferences, governments, during regional preparatory meetings, are entitled to place on the table for discussion issues they consider relevant. Such issues are then discussed and negotiated in a lengthy process that ultimately reflects a global consensus in the final document. Usually agreement is reached in the last hour of the final day.

The decision by the U.S. and Israeli governments to leave the conference before its conclusion was regrettable because it occurred during intense efforts to remove the unacceptable language and make the event a success. In the end, all anti-Semitic language was successfully removed, but the terrible attacks of 9/11 three days later understandably prevented a considered appraisal of the Durban outcome.

Now, more than two years later, I find that many people want to understand what happened in Durban. Yet, few here in the United States are aware of the real progress that was actually made. The final declaration and program of action are powerful tools for lobbying governments, educating people, empowering civil societies, and establishing frameworks for dialogue. Their specific calls and strategies for countering anti-Semitism; challenging rising xenophobia; and protecting minorities, indigenous peoples, migrants, and other vulnerable groups should be used and not disregarded out of hand.

Equally important, Durban created an opportunity for victim groups around the world, many of whom had been without a voice on the world stage, to articulate their concerns and engage their governments in a new and powerful way. Groups representing the Roma, the African-descendant communities in Latin America, migrants, the Dalits of India, and many other marginalized peoples found in Durban an energizing place to forge new alliances and strengthen grassroots efforts to address the problems they faced at home.

Perhaps what people in the U.S. most want to know is, what lessons can we learn from the Durban experience in countering anti-Semitism today? I would say, first, that governments everywhere must acknowledge that anti-Semitism is a virulent form of racism and that anti-Semitic acts need to be seen as violations of international human rights law. Its governments need systematically to monitor and report on hate crimes and to adopt aggressive measures to prosecute those who are responsible.

Second, I believe we must all be vigilant in distinguishing legitimate criticism of acts by the Israeli security forces—which have raised serious and legitimate human rights concerns—from the anti-Semitism that masquerades as concern. While rightly condemning suicide attacks and other assaults against civilians, the global community must set and honor clear lines in the debate about current Israeli practices with respect to the Palestinians.

Supporters of Israel need to recognize that criticisms of Israeli policies and practices are not in and of themselves anti-Semitic. Many human rights groups here and elsewhere are sharply—and I believe rightly—critical of some of Israel's practices, such as targeted killings, based on the application of universally accepted international human rights norms. The Jewish community should engage in this discussion and use its influence to challenge the government of Israel whenever its policies and security forces violate these international standards.

At the same time, those who advocate for the rights of Palestinians must ensure that their criticisms and related actions do not become broadside attacks against Jews and the Jewish state. It is at this point that they become racist. The conflict in the

Middle East between Israelis and Palestinians—and by extension much of the Arab world—will become even harder to address if the rhetoric continues in this way, if anger against Israel continues to spill over into broader patterns of antagonism against Jews, and if the speech devolves into outright racism and calling into question Israel's right to exist.

And just as there has been a sharp rise in anti-Semitism, so also, in the aftermath of 9/11, there has been a sharp increase in Islamophobia and anti-Arab sentiment. Families and even whole communities live in fear or endure new levels of hostility. Students are unable to obtain visas, academics cannot attend conferences, and people worry about traveling out of the country and being unable to return.

All this leads me to a final point that I believe we must look at together in an open and honest way. There are some in this country and elsewhere who suggest that human rights concerns, including the specific issues of discrimination I have been raising this evening, might get in the way of winning the peace or the war against terrorism. But there can be no stable peace, no true human security, without human rights and real public participation. There can be no true enjoyment of human rights by all where some are excluded by discrimination and prejudice.

Can the future be different? Can we come to expect greater shared responsibility for realizing the rights which we proclaim as being basic to a life of dignity for every individual?

Let me share with you the deep sense of hope and encouragement I experienced just last week in Ireland. In a hotel near the border with Northern Ireland, I had been invited to address a conference of local community groups from areas such as North Belfast and North Dublin, where local people over several months had been working through a rights-based approach to their problems. The theme of their conference was participation and the practice of rights in making connections and owning outcomes. I met senior citizens from both communities and women from the Shankill Protestant and the Falls Catholic women's centers in Belfast. I met youth workers, former prisoners, and community activists, all engaged in a conscious attempt to relate human rights standards to their local experience in poor housing estates and inner city environments. In the process, they had forged close friendships across the religious and political divides of the past. They were living Eleanor Roosevelt's philosophy that if human rights are to matter at all, they must matter in small places close to home. "It isn't easy," they told me, "but the experience has bonded us together."

I am also encouraged by examples of innovative thinking here in the United States. Some of you may be aware of a report issued last year by the Migration Policy Institute, titled *America's Challenge*, which, among other recommendations, proposes the creation of an independent national commission on integration to address the specific challenges of national unity presented by post-September 11 events and actions. The report recommends that such a commission should be guided by the principle that the long-term interests of the nation lie in policies that strengthen the social and political fabric by "… weaving into it, rather than pulling out of it, all immigrant and ethnic communities. In the post-September 11 world, this means paying special attention to the experiences of Arab and Muslim communities, as well as to South Asian communities who are sometimes mistaken to be Muslim or Arab."

The report calls for new policies that consciously and systematically prevent stigmatization of Muslim and Arab communities and actively see them as adding to the social, political, and security strengths of the country. It highlights the importance of educational instruction about Islam and Muslims in schools and workplaces and encourages interfaith dialogue at national and local community levels. The report points out that promoting tolerance and pluralism is a huge challenge.

Like any other ethnic or religious minority, the Muslim population alone cannot dispel the prejudices about its communities and religion. In the end, it is up to all of us.

I conclude with a simple truth, which President Sadat understood so well: whether our world becomes a more brutal or a more peaceful place rests in our own hands. Human rights have become the world's common benchmark for justice, but they have yet to become our common framework for action. In giving his life for peace, Anwar Sadat gave inspiration to generations to come. Yes, the challenges ahead are formidable, the familiar catalog of problems and future obstacles remains to be faced. Yes, we have a long road to travel before human rights will be secured for all. But I am convinced that this is a time when civil society worldwide can make its voice heard as never before.

If we can overcome doubts and fears, if we can build on shared values and learn to recognize ourselves in the other, this century can, after such a tragic beginning, become one of human development and human security for all—a century of human rights and peace.

Thank you, Dr. Sadat, for your vision in keeping alive your husband's ideals.

8

JAMES BAKER III

Ladies and gentlemen, I cannot but believe that if President Sadat were with us today, he would be amazed by the recent changes in the Middle East. This is a time of great opportunity for resolving issues that have festered for decades. In early January, President Bush said, "I believe democracy can take hold in parts of the world that have been condemned to tyranny. And I believe when democracies take hold, it leads to peace."

The president's assertion was met with skepticism by some and with downright mockery by others. Now, however, in April, a wind of change is blowing in the Middle East. Among Arab reformers, there is a belief that this wind has blown down a metaphorical Berlin Wall in the Middle East.

Criticism of the president has ebbed and skeptics are now asking themselves a simple question, "Could Bush be right?" Is freedom, as President Bush announced last month, on the march in the Middle East?

Only time will tell if there will be a flowering of democracy along the banks of the Nile and the Euphrates. There are many hurdles yet to overcome in a region that has been prone to heartbreaks and setbacks.

However, it is clear that something dramatic has happened in the Middle East since the invasion of Iraq. Citizens are taking up the gritty responsibility of self-determination. Listen to how U.S. Army Lt. Col. Mark Martins describes the effects of the successful Iraqi election. "Democracy," Martins said, "is not a luxury car. It is an all-terrain vehicle and good for fighting insurgency." He is right. What is happening isn't always pretty, but it's sometimes very effective.

Perhaps nothing better represents what has happened in the Middle East than the Cedar Revolution in Lebanon. People power is changing things in Lebanon, much as it did in Ukraine months ago during the Orange Revolution. As a result of the pressure, Syrian leaders have promised to pull out all of their military and intelligence forces from Lebanon by the end of the month, before the nationwide elections scheduled for late May.

And the development in Lebanon is only one part of a shaking-up of the chess board in that region of the world. Just consider what else has happened during the past two years in the Muslim world:

• Libya has given up its WMD program.

- Afghanistan, freed from the Taliban, has conducted a successful election.
- Iraq experienced a 60-percent voter turnout for their election in January. While the jury is still out on the future of that country, the election was a clear and compelling example of the exercise of democracy.
- Palestinians conducted a free and fair election in January when they chose Abu Mazen to replace Yasir Arafat, a revolutionary who never successfully made the transition to being a popular leader.
- Egypt said it will now hold multicandidate elections for president—not just one candidate.

While many factors have undoubtedly contributed to these transformations, I am biased enough to believe that American leadership heads the list, starting with our involvement first in Afghanistan and then in Iraq. It is becoming increasingly evident that toppling the regime of Saddam Hussein has contributed to a growing impulse in other countries toward reform.

Last month, King Abdullah of Jordan recognized this evolution that is occurring. At first, he said, Arab countries feared that reform was going to be imposed from the outside. But now, he said, reform is no longer taboo. It is being openly debated in the Arab world. Partly at least, as a result of U.S. engagement in Iraq and Afghanistan, pressure for reform is bubbling up from the grassroots in other countries.

Assisting this grassroots effort is the proliferation of satellite television and of the Internet, which are effectively spreading information and ideas.

Increasingly, it is difficult for governments to control the news that their people receive. As Nadim Shehadi of the Centre for Lebanese Studies at Oxford University recently said, "The regimes that are built on the principle of controlling information—like the old Eastern Europe-style of controlling information and controlling thought, if you like—are not sustainable anymore. They are in a time warp."

The new technologies appear to be having the same effect on Middle Easterners as televised news had on Americans during the Vietnam War. Satellite television and the Internet very well could be the voice of democracy for the Middle East.

Of course, despite the encouraging trends, many problems remain that will require leadership, attention, and involvement.

Among them is the need to use public diplomacy in the Muslim world to better explain U.S. policies. Because a decades-long battle for the hearts and minds of the Islamic world has just started, it is critical that the Muslim world understand that we have no problems with Muslims in general—only with extremists who advocate, promote, and execute violence.

In the broader Middle East, there are three specific challenges facing American policymakers. The first challenge is fostering the emergency of a stable, representative Iraq at peace with its neighbors. Whatever your views of the wisdom of the war were originally, a hasty U.S. departure at this point would diminish our credibility around the world and embolden insurgents.

Furthermore, there are grounds for guarded optimism. Reconstruction is going forward. Political parties are organizing. Iraqi security forces are being trained. Progress may be slower than many had hoped, but it is occurring.

Most importantly, Iraqis disproved critics who didn't believe the country could successfully conduct the election for a 275-seat general assembly on January 30. Iraq experienced a 60-percent turnout among voters who risked their lives to go to the polls. Since then, General John P. Abizaid, head of U.S. Central Command, has recently said that he believes we have gone from a primarily military environment to a primarily political one.

So the purple finger may yet replace the car bomb as the most effective agent of change in Iraq.

Still, we cannot and should not underestimate the difficulties ahead as Iraq prepares for a December target date of establishing a working constitution and a permanent government. An important hurdle was cleared last Wednesday when the general assembly broke a ten-week political deadlock to appoint a president and two vice presidents. And a day later, Ibrahim Jaafari, a physician and long-time leader of one of Iraq's major Shiite religious parties, was selected to serve as prime minister.

But, until a permanent government is finally in place—and possibly longer—we can fully expect attacks on Iraq and coalition forces to continue, especially in Sunni areas. Civil war remains a possibility, remote I think, but a possibility. And neighboring countries could meddle in Iraqi affairs, feeding ethnic and religious strife.

Given these realities, a protracted U.S. military presence appears unavoidable. But it was encouraging to see U.S. military leaders say that the training of Iraqi forces is going well enough to consider major reductions in U.S. forces by this time next year.

Preventing Iran from acquiring nuclear weapons is the second specific challenge confronting the United States in this region. It will also create immense pressure on other countries—Saudi Arabia chief among them—to do likewise, setting off destabilizing regional arms races. Not least, a nuclear Iran will raise the risk that deadly technology or materials might find their way into the hands of terrorists bent on using them against the United States.

The United States, and the international community, must insist on absolute adherence to all commitments regarding nuclear weapons. Iran has been a flagrant offender in this regard.

President Bush is right to embrace a multilateral effort to try to halt progress by Iran to acquire nuclear weapons. And he is right to use a mix of carrots and sticks in our approach to this challenge.

The European Union is currently taking the lead in negotiations with Tehran aimed at extending Iran's temporary halt to its nuclear enrichment program into a permanent, verifiable freeze. We are now working with them, thereby making possible the carrot of potential accession to the World Trade Organization.

But we must also be prepared to use sticks. And there are, of course, sticks that fall short of full-fledged military action, like political and economic sanctions by the United Nations Security Council. Iran, like North Korea, has a track record of playing cat and mouse when it comes to its nuclear programs. To be blunt, simple declarations of intent are worthless.

And so, any agreements that are concluded must include provisions for international inspections—any time and any place.

Third, and finally, but most importantly, the United States must work to promote Arab-Israeli peace.

Two events—the reelection of President Bush and the emergence of a new Palestinian leadership in the wake of Arafat's death—have created a unique opportunity for negotiating peace between Arabs and Israelis.

I believe that this current window of opportunity is similar to the one that existed in 1991. Then, Washington seized the moment to convene the Madrid Peace Conference, the first-ever face-to-face meeting of Israel and all of its Arab neighbors.

Today, the president should, of course, continue with his goal of spreading democracy in the Middle East. And the January election in Iraq was a critical step in the right direction. But it is imperative that the president also actively promote peace

between Israelis and Arabs—something which I know he wants to do.

Stability in Iraq and peace between Palestinians and Israelis can be pursued at the same time. In fact, addressing the latter improves the chances of attaining the former. The road to peace doesn't run through just Jerusalem or Baghdad. That is a false choice. Today it arguably runs through both.

So the real question is how to take advantage of this window of opportunity to achieve that peace. Specifically, what steps should be taken? Who needs to do what?

An important first step has already occurred—Israel now has a negotiating partner on the Palestinian side. That partner emerged on January 9th when Abu Mazen was elected as the Palestinian president. He has displayed a commitment to end the violence and resume negotiations with Israelis. He has cracked down on extremists and used very conciliatory language toward Israel.

Israeli prime minister Ariel Sharon has responded in kind, releasing Palestinian prisoners and reducing the area of West Bank territory falling within Israel's new security barrier. When Sharon and Abu Mazen have met, they have seemed to understand one another.

Now, Palestinian officials must continue to clearly and unequivocally renounce terror as a means of achieving a political result—and call upon their supporters to do likewise. And those Palestinians should commit themselves to an unequivocal, good-faith effort to crack down on terrorist groups targeting Israel.

In exchange, Israel should resume substantive negotiations for peace without requiring that all terrorist activities cease in advance. To require the absence of any terrorist act in advance simply empowers the terrorists themselves to prevent the resumption of peace negotiations.

The United States should itself clearly embrace and articulate the unequivocal, good-faith standard for the resumption of dialogue. The United States should further prevail upon Israel to freeze settlement activity in the occupied territories during the resumption of peace negotiations, as called for by the road map. Washington should do everything that it can to encourage both sides to resume substantive negotiations. And it should serve, where necessary, as a direct participant in the talks, offering suggestions, brokering compromises, and extending assurances.

Finally, the administration must make it unambiguously clear to Israel that while Prime Minister Sharon's planned withdrawal from Gaza is a positive initiative, it cannot be simply the first step in a unilateral process leading to the creation of Palestinian Bantustans in the West Bank.

I believe that the president made this point when he met Monday with Sharon in Crawford, Texas. He also publicly criticized Israel's plans for new housing units that would establish an unbroken presence from Jerusalem to the settlement of Ma'ale Adumim as being in contravention of Israel's obligations under the road map.

In February, the James Baker Institute for Public Policy at Rice University released a guide for the successful implementation of Israeli and Palestinian commitments and a return to the road map. We called the policy paper the street map to the road map, and it recommends that the Bush administration assist the parties in turning unilateral action into a comprehensive multilateral action program that leads to the renewal of bilateral Israeli-Palestinian negotiations.

The street map says that the task of American leadership should be to

- define the strategic direction of the road map implementation process by encouraging both sides to reach a cessation of violence as the necessary framework for security action, encouraging the Palestinian Authority to consolidate security reform, and encouraging Israel to implement the understandings reached regarding unilateral disengagement.
- assist in capacity building supporting Palestinian governmental and security reform and Israeli disengagement. This will create a sustainable security system respected by the population.
- lead an internal effort supporting Palestinian economic rehabilitation in the West Bank and Gaza Strip to accompany Israeli disengagement. This could include expert and

financial support for the creation of a formal Israeli-Palestinian border regime to operate along the 1967 border.

- provide safety nets for crisis situations. These can include creating and maintaining a crisis management mechanism to keep the focus of the parties on the peace process in spite of actions by spoiler elements. The same verification mechanism that is employed to monitor compliance with agreements by the parties should be used to verify that the actions of spoiler elements are being addressed by the parties.
- use the unique capital of U.S. leadership to ensure an adequate response to compliance and noncompliance by the parties.

Fostering the Arab-Israeli peace process will, of course, continue to test American resolve, patience, and leadership. But, in the end, the United States cannot create peace in the Middle East. Only Arabs and Israelis can do that. Washington's role is to help them. As the United States continues with that role, above all else, we need to remember five historical truisms about this dispute.

First, there is a catch-22 regarding the issue and that is this: Israel will never enjoy security as long as she occupies the territories, and the Palestinians will never achieve their dream of living in peace in their own state as long as Israel lacks security. It is a tragic version of the old chicken-or-egg question.

Second, there is no military solution because neither side will win the conflict by dominating the other.

Third, a political process and dialogue are essential in the Arab-Israeli dispute. Whenever the political process breaks down, there will be violence on the ground.

Fourth, hard-liners on both sides have been the biggest impediment to a solution, including Arabs who won't accept Israel's right to exist and Israelis who want to keep all the land.

And fifth, only the United States can serve as an effective mediator because of the country's special relationship with Israel.

In conclusion, ladies and gentlemen, it is clear that the United States must and will continue to play a key role in the Middle East, and we have a variety of tools to address the challenges presented there.

There will be times when we must go it alone. We should not forget that the surest and best test of a great power is its ability to act unilaterally to protect its vital interests—when that is required. In dealing with shadowy, stateless groups like al-Qaeda, we face a radically different adversary. Preemptive military action against terrorist groups and states that harbor them is not merely justifiable. Sometimes, it is imperative.

However, if indeed we live in a unipolar world, it is important that America not be viewed as an empire. It is not and does not intend to be.

Indeed, our track-record—from rebuilding Western Europe and East Asia after World War II to peacefully concluding the Cold War—proves that we have a history of exercising our power in ways that advance the human condition.

I would submit to you that the United States rightly views itself as the final guarantor of international security, the chief engine of economic growth, and the historic champion of democratic values around the world. But it wants and needs the cooperation of an international community that cherishes freedom and free markets.

Ladies and gentlemen, I am optimistic that a better world is possible for our children and grandchildren and for those in the Middle East.

But a brighter future will require leadership. And I don't just mean American leadership. I mean leadership by all those of good will—Arab and Israeli alike—who would rather look forward with hope than back with bitterness.

Anwar Sadat was such a leader—a man of vision, courage, and deep love for his country. The Middle East will need more like him in the challenging months and years ahead.

9

MOHAMED ELBARADEI

Humanity's quest for peace is not confined to one region. The situation in the Middle East may be the most acute, but the search for security is still the major concern for many people and nations.

Today I will begin by looking at the international security landscape, then focus on the Middle East as a case in point. The current security picture is paradoxical. As a writer in the *Financial Times* aptly put it, "The world has rarely been more peaceful or felt so insecure."

According to a recent report on human security, there has been a sharp decline since the early 1990s in civil wars and other forms of armed conflict. The number of refugees has also gone down, and human rights abuses have decreased. These statistics indicate that the world is becoming more peaceful.

Yet at the same time, the collective sense of insecurity is higher than at any time before, because the forces that drive insecurity remain persistent and pervasive. These drivers of insecurity fit into four categories.

First, poverty, and poverty-related insecurities, for the billions who lack access to reliable food supplies, safe drinking water, adequate health care, and modern energy supplies. This is the rawest form of insecurity—a reality for 40 percent of our fellow human beings who live on the edge of survival on less than $2 per day.

I was delighted earlier this month to see the Norwegian Nobel Committee give explicit recognition to this linkage between poverty and other forms of insecurity by awarding the 2006 Nobel Peace Prize to Muhammad Yunus and Grameen Bank. The citation read, in part, "Lasting peace cannot be achieved unless large population groups find ways in which to break out of poverty," and later, "Development from below also serves to advance democracy and human rights."

A second category is the lack of good governance—not infrequently linked to poverty—which ranges from corruption to severely repressive regimes whose hallmark is egregious human rights abuses. Democracy recently has made remarkable strides, particularly in Eastern Europe and Latin America. But many tyrants remain in the Middle East and other regions.

A third driver of insecurity is the sense of injustice that results from the imbalance between the haves and have-nots, the sharp contrasts in wealth and power that we see between the North and the South. This sense of injustice is magnified by the perception that the sanctity of human life is not equally valued, that society grieves the loss of life in the developed world far more than it grieves the greater loss of life in places like Darfur or Iraq, or, for that matter, in Congo, where nearly four million people have lost their lives in civil war since 1996.

Fourth is the artificial polarization along religious or ethnic lines. This is a centuries-old phenomenon, but it continues to flare up, recently leading some to worry about a clash of civilizations between Muslims and the West. In my view, it is an utter mistake to think that these tensions arise from clashing religious values. But for people who suffer gross inequities—many of them in the Muslim world—it is easy to be convinced that their suffering is due to religious or ethnic prejudice instead of the real causes that have existed throughout history: warring people and nations, fighting over power and resources. This conviction can make them more likely to seek refuge in distorted views of religion or ethnicity in order to channel their rage and redress their grievances.

In a few regions—including not only the Middle East but also South Asia and the Korean Peninsula—conflicts arising from a mixture of insecurities have been left to fester for decades. The longer these conflicts and insecurities ferment unaddressed, the greater the sense of injustice and humiliation. It is in these same regions where, over time, we have seen the rise of extremism and the constant threat of internal strife, interstate wars, and the efforts by states to seek weapons of mass destruction.

The human security picture would not be complete without factoring in the impact of globalization. Modern society is interdependent as never before. This interdependence is a double-edged sword; it provides opportunities to address these problems more effectively, but it can also accentuate them. Television, the Internet, and ease of travel have made it easier to exchange ideas, expand trade, and interact with each other. But these and other tools of globalization, including greater access to advanced technology, have arguably also made it easier for extremist groups to operate.

Against this backdrop, it should be apparent why conventional concepts of security—rooted in the protection of national borders and old concepts of sovereignty—are no longer adequate. Most of the drivers of insecurity I have mentioned are without borders. If a new extremist group emerges in the Middle East, it makes me worry. If a new civil war breaks out in an African state, I will be disturbed. Not only because we are all members of the same human family, but also because of the probability that each of these developments will affect me sooner or later.

In other words, the modern age demands that we think in terms of human security, a concept of security that is people-centered and without borders. A concept that acknowledges the inherent linkages between economic and social development, respect for human rights, and peace.

This is the basis on which we must reengineer security.

While national security is just as relevant as before, the strategies to achieve it must be much more global than in the past, and our remedies must be centered on the welfare of the individual and not simply focused on the security of the state.

Until we understand and act accordingly, we will not have either national or international security.

With these concepts of human security as our benchmark, how well do our national and international institutions perform?

In the broadest sense, the United Nations and its system of organizations have a remarkable record of achievement. We have had no world wars in more than sixty years. UN bodies have succeeded in setting norms and overseeing many important aspects of our life—such as labor relations, global health, civil aviation, food and agriculture, and trade.

Despite these achievements, however, the system often falls short in addressing threats to international peace and security. When faced with such threats, the outcomes are neither certain nor consistent.

The Security Council, and the United Nations in general, can point to some success stories as a peacemaker in terms of conflict prevention and conflict resolution and as a peacekeeper in the aftermath of conflicts. It is through the consistent efforts of the UN that scores of nations have achieved independence after centuries of colonialism. And sixteen UN peacekeeping missions are currently operating in almost every corner of the world, containing conflicts and maintaining the peace.

But to understand the urgency of reforming our system for maintaining international peace and security, we must also look critically at situations where it has not been able to adequately fulfill its function. I would mention three aspects in that regard.

First, the Security Council—as well as regional organizations and institutions—have often been unable to intervene in a timely manner in humanitarian crises and in cases of gross violations of human rights. The most glaring example is perhaps the 1994 genocide in Rwanda, in which roughly one million people were slaughtered in a period of one hundred days, despite advance intelligence and international media coverage as the atrocities unfolded. The ongoing tragedy in Darfur is another painful case in point.

Second, we have allowed some conflicts to fester for decades, with devastating effects. The Palestinian people, for example, have been subjected to thirty-nine years of occupation, leading inevitably to increased polarization and militancy. These conflicts—like other more recent conflicts in Iraq, Afghanistan, and Somalia—could be solved. They persist because the international community, despite intermittent efforts, has not made the necessary investments nor mustered the resolve needed to end these conflicts.

Third, a number of the central tenets of international law—which have been painstakingly developed and on which our modern civilization depends—have been challenged or undermined in recent years. Consider a few examples. Civilians are supposed to be protected during times of war. Weapons that kill indiscriminately are supposed to be prohibited. The authority to use force is supposed to be centralized in the Security Council, except in the case of a state's self-defense, and then only until the Security Council intervenes. And the council is supposed to be responsible for putting an immediate end to violence. With these principles at the core of the international security system, perhaps it is not surprising that many saw a dangerous and disturbing precedent in the council's recent reluctance to bring the fighting in Lebanon to a prompt end, despite the daily loss of innocent lives.

But with all the vulnerabilities in our security structures, I believe the system can be fixed. For reform to be effective, three things must occur.

First, as I have already suggested, we must view both the problems and their solutions through the lens of human security. The international community must rise and come to the defense of the life, freedom, and dignity of every individual or group, whether the aggressor is an occupying force or a ruthless dictator. This is not simply a moral obligation. We should be aware that even from a utilitarian viewpoint, we will not achieve national or international security unless every one of us is able to live in freedom and dignity. The sovereign rights of the individual must take precedence over the sovereignty of the state. It is therefore imperative to put in practice the international community's responsibility to protect against genocide, ethnic cleansing, and other gross violations of human rights, as referred to in the UN World Summit in 2005.

If our strategies are focused on achieving human security, then we will quickly see the advantage of finding solutions through dialogue and negotiation rather than through confrontation and the use of force. In bygone eras, when a country could view itself as a self-sufficient entity, war may have been a reasonable strategy for protecting its interests. But in an interdependent world, my enemy today could very well be my partner tomorrow. We will have to share resources, combat common environmental and health issues, and interact with each other on many levels. By settling differences in a fair manner that balances the interests of all parties, we create the necessary environment for lasting peace and future cooperation.

Similarly, if we are committed to achieving human security, we will seek collective solutions. If security for one country is achieved in a way that results in insecurity for another, the system will eventually break.

If our focus is on achieving human security, then we will seek to correct the global imbalance in wealth and power through a system of distributive justice. We will ensure that the tools of globalization are used to enhance the lot of poorer nations and peoples, rather than widening the gap between rich and poor. The least-developed countries will be viewed not as weaker neighbors to be exploited but as a wealth of human resources to be tapped for mutual benefit. By establishing an equitable and generous system for finance and trade and creating a level playing field, these less privileged can be given the opportunity to trade their way to development.

Second, our security mechanisms and institutions must be reformed. They must evolve to match current threats. To that end, we cannot leave existing vulnerabilities unaddressed.

At the IAEA [International Atomic Energy Agency], for example, we are working to address a number of vulnerabilities that exist under the Nuclear Non-Proliferation Treaty. One such important vulnerability is that we have at times ignored the linkage between nuclear nonproliferation and nuclear disarmament. In an environment in which we have continuing reliance on nuclear weapons by some countries, in which scant progress is being made on nuclear disarmament and in which efforts to bring a Comprehensive Nuclear Test Ban Treaty into force have been stymied for years, the recent nuclear weapon test by North Korea, while inexcusable, was nonetheless predictable. Inaction, too, has its price.

A much needed evolution is for our security institutions to be more agile in conflict prevention and conflict resolution. The old adage in medicine says an ounce of prevention is worth a pound of cure, and so it is with responding to security threats. If multilateral and regional approaches to conflict prevention are viewed as inherently sluggish, the alternative—unilateral action—may seem more attractive. That is a lesson that must be unlearned. Multilateral and regional mechanisms must become effective and timely in their capacity to preempt and contain crises.

Reform to institutions and mechanisms can be prompted by the engagement of civil society and by putting human security first. To paraphrase a famous quote, human security is too important to be left to governments. A good example is the process that led to the Ottawa convention banning antipersonnel landmines. Using the pressure of public opinion, non-governmental organizations and members of civil society made clear that these landmines could not be tolerated as a weapon of war. In my view, the same argument is even more valid for nuclear weapons. It is unconscionable to continue living under the nightmare of annihilation through the use of nuclear weapons, intentional or otherwise.

Third, we must commit to resolve longstanding conflicts. It is not enough to engage intermittently or in a piecemeal fashion. Which brings me to the Middle East, where a number of the drivers of insecurity I have referred to continue to feed on each other.

A case in point is the Arab-Israeli conflict, which at its most basic level comes down to two passionate peoples claiming the same piece of land. These claims are rooted in religious belief and differing views of history. The sense of entitlement is fervent on both sides. For the Jewish people, reclaiming their Promised Land symbolizes a positive end to centuries of pogroms that culminated in the Holocaust. The Palestinians, on the other hand, cannot conceive why the Jewish question had to be settled at their expense and why, after living there for one or two millennia, their land had to be divided into two states.

Israel lives with a constant sense of insecurity in a neighborhood in which it is largely boycotted and isolated. In less than sixty years, there have been four wars, two intifadas, and many smaller conflicts involving the loss of innocent lives. Only two countries—Egypt and Jordan—formally recognize and have peace agreements with Israel. The peace that has existed for most of that time has more or less been a Cold Peace, a formal peace only minimally supported by interaction between people. And the wisdom of that peace is often called into question by critical voices in the two countries, as well as in the Arab world at large, in the face of the continued Israeli occupation of the Palestinian territories. Meanwhile, many of the Palestinian refugees have for decades lived in squalor—unable to own land, for example, or to obtain proper travel documents—conditions that have added to their humiliation.

Today, the Arabs continue to show little readiness to accept Israel as long as there is no resolution to the Palestinian issue. Israel, on the other hand, continues to consolidate its occupation in the face of its perceived existential threat and the absence of peace in the region. This is the catch-22 James Baker referred to last year, from this podium, as a tragic version of the old chicken-or-egg question.

If the recent history of the Middle East teaches us nothing else, it should teach us that these conflicts cannot be solved through military force. Every type of violence has been tried, from occupation by force and outright military confrontation to oppression, terrorism, and targeted assassination without a single instance that brought either party closer to peace or security. Each act of violence in the region only begets more violence and added insecurity.

The solution will not lie in reconstructing history. And it will not lie in redressing all past injustices. If we are to solve the central conflict of the Middle East, we must begin by looking forward, not backward, by being ready to reconcile and recognize mutual rights, and above all by finding in our hearts the ability to forgive.

One thing is clear: the status quo is not acceptable. The threat of other regional states acquiring nuclear weapons or other weapons of mass destruction will continue to be a grave international concern. The rise of extremist groups originating in the Middle East—and the ease with which they recruit in the region—will continue to be high on the list of international insecurities. The dependency of many countries on Middle East oil and natural gas will continue to add a dimension of global economic risk to any conflict. And when events in the region give rise to perceived religious and cultural divisions between the Muslim world and the West, the repercussions will continue to be felt everywhere.

In spite of this rather gloomy state of affairs, I believe there is a glimmer of hope. Lost in the middle of all this conflict and violence are two major psychological breakthroughs.

The first is the readiness of the Arab countries, as expressed in the Arab League Summit of March 2002, to have full normal relations with Israel, provided that Israel withdraws to the June 1967 borders, ensures a just solution for Palestinian refugees, and recognizes the establishment of a Palestinian state. This is a far cry from the Arab summit decision of 1967 in Khartoum, which formulated its policy toward Israel as no peace, no recognition, and no negotiation.

The second is the recognition by Israel of the right of the Palestinians to have their own independent state. This is also a far cry from Israel's previous position, which for many years questioned the right of the Palestinians to independence or even their separate identity. In June 2002, President George Bush articulated for the first time the formal support of the United States for a Palestinian state, laying out the principles of what would be called the road map to achieve that goal.

For security in the Middle East to be realized will naturally require more than just finding a so-lution to the Israeli-Palestinian issue. The need to achieve stability in Iraq and Lebanon; to normalize relations with Iran; and to address pressing issues of development, governance, and modernity throughout the region are only a few of the substantial challenges that must be dealt with.

But if the Palestinian question were to be resolved, a decades-old burden of Arab-Israeli tensions would be lifted that would improve immeasurably our ability to deal with these and other challenges.

I would like to offer, in closing, a few suggestions on how to move forward. By this I do not mean a new road map or what a final accord should look like. In fact, what is ironic about this long-standing conflict is that the basic outline and even most of the details about how to resolve the conflict have already been worked out since 1967—in Security Council resolutions 242 (1967) and 338 (1973) and in numerous initiatives that aimed to give effect to the principles outlined in these resolutions.

Just earlier this month, the International Crisis Group published a statement signed by 137 prominent leaders from every corner of the globe entitled "Towards a Comprehensive Settlement of the Arab-Israeli Conflict." The statement made clear the goal of such a settlement: "security and full recognition to the State of Israel within internationally recognized borders, an end to the occupation for the Palestinian people in a viable independent, sovereign state, and the return of lost land to Syria." And, I should add, a just settlement for the Palestinian refugees who have been living in a state of uncertainty for two generations and now number more than four million.

As the International Crisis Group statement noted, "Everyone has lost in this conflict except the extremists throughout the world who prosper on the rage that it continues to provoke."

I do believe, however, that a solution to this conflict is within our grasp, provided that the conditions are created to enable this solution to come into being. To extend the metaphor Mr. Baker used last year, if the parties involved can look beyond the pointless question of which comes first, the chicken or the egg, perhaps the peace process can finally get the needed period of incubation and can give birth to a new era in the Middle East.

The first key to success, in my view, will be to start from the endpoint—in other words, to begin with the blueprint of the settlement, and then work backward toward the details of implementation. As the International Crisis Group statement suggested, this could be the focus of a new international conference, at which all the elements of a comprehensive peace agreement would be mapped, and momentum generated for detailed negotiations.

There are two reasons to start from the endpoint and work backward. First, because there is already a great deal of agreement on what that blueprint would look like, agreement is not far away. Second, once the blueprint is clearly in place, highlighting the benefits to all parties—the light at the end of the tunnel, so to speak—it should draw attention away from contentious issues and provide incentives for mutual accommodation.

The second key condition is steady commitment by all parties. To date, a key failure has been the tendency of the international community to work on this issue by fits and starts. This must change. The resolution of this conflict is too urgent, its impact too important, to allow it to be sidetracked by changes in leadership or to be derailed by intervening violence. By allowing the process to be sidetracked or derailed, we only further arm the hard-liners.

As we know from other cases, such as Northern Ireland, successful negotiation in the cause of peace requires the investment of considerable time and influence. The peoples of the Middle East must develop the needed trust in the process. For that to happen, they must regain faith that the outside world cares and is ready to give peace in their region the sustained support and engagement it deserves. This investment will result in arming the moderates.

In parallel with the dialogue on the peace process, there should be a dialogue on regional security. This discussion should cover the elimination of weapons of mass destruction, limitations on conventional weapons, and an array of confidence-building measures. These security dimensions have yet to be fully discussed as part of the peace process; however, they are essential to undergird peace in a region that has been beset for over a hundred years by wars, hatred, and suffering.

Another important condition is that all parties with a stake in the solution be engaged in a dialogue. Much of the process will involve changing the mind-set on both sides away from stereotyping and past grievances toward mutual acceptance and future cooperation. For this mind-set to change, dialogue must be seen as the only alternative—dialogue conducted on the basis of mutual respect.

It is time to move away from thinking of dialogue as a reward for good behavior—and to recognize it instead as an essential tool for effecting such behavior.

True peace requires dialogue and interaction between peoples to enable them to know, understand, and accept one another. The peoples of the Middle East are nearly all the children of Abraham—distant cousins, if you like—estranged by decades of retribution. Here we have suffered from a more fundamental catch-22: the less we interact, the more we believe in negative stereotypes; and the more we believe in negative stereotypes, the less we interact. Ironically, deep in our hearts, we all know that we share the same core values: the desire to have a chance to live with our families in peace, freedom, and dignity.

But these shared values will only emerge through interaction. The political framework must certainly be settled, but in the end, it is normal human interaction that will become the basis for an enduring peace.

Finally, I think it is important to mention the religious overtones that at times enter the debate over a Middle East solution. Christians, Jews, and Muslims all have sites in the Holy Land that are considered sacred. Like any other aspect of cultural diversity, these religions should be treated with mutual deference.

However, the effort by some parties to inject a religious dimension into the Israeli-Palestinian issue should be resisted by all means because policies rooted in religious beliefs leave no room for compromise.

Nearly thirty years ago, President Sadat's visit to Jerusalem was a leap of faith to shatter deeply entrenched psychological barriers of fear, distrust, and rejection. His achievement of peace with Israel proved that peace in the Middle East could be realized, no matter how difficult. Unfortunately, the circumstances at that time did not lend themselves to the fulfillment of Sadat's wider vision.

It is to the great credit of Mrs. Sadat that she has continued to carry out his legacy, to speak out in the cause of peace, and to act as a role model for Egyptian and Arab women.

May we have the courage, wisdom, and determination to achieve President Sadat's dream for a just and lasting peace in our troubled region.

CONCLUDING THOUGHTS

AMERICA AND ARAB-ISRAELI PEACE, 1997–2009

AARON DAVID MILLER

If Anwar Sadat were alive today, he would have much to celebrate. He would have taken great pride in the tributes paid to him in this volume by so distinguished a group of diplomatic luminaries and in the lecture series that bears his name. More important, he would have looked with enormous satisfaction on the fact that his successor Hosni Mubarak had followed his path, that Jordan had become the second Arab state to conclude a peace treaty with Israel, and that most of the Arab world under the leadership of Saudi King Abdullah's 2002 initiative grasped the importance of reaching out to Israel. If prescience is the hallmark of the statesman, then Sadat was prescient; he could see well before its time that peacemaking, not war, was the pathway to regional stability and prosperity.

Still, the Egyptian president, reviewing the regional landscape, would also have been worried about what he surveyed. Sadat would have agonized over the plight and suffering of the Palestinian people, particularly in the wake of the 2008–09 Gaza war, and been fearful of the rise of Islamic extrem-ism and the growing power and influence of Hamas, Hezbollah, and Iran. Al-Qaeda's attacks on America would have shocked him to the core.

So, too, Sadat would have likely despaired about the state of American diplomacy. Had he surveyed the last ten years of peacemaking efforts, encompassing roughly Bill Clinton's second term and much of George W. Bush's presidency, he would have looked at a dysfunctional phase in America's diplomacy, one of opportunities missed and those never seized at all. Sadat would have despaired, particularly because he had placed enormous trust and faith in the power of the United States. Indeed, having seized the initiative on the battlefield in October 1973, Sadat created an opening for American diplomacy and then helped fill it. Two of the men in this volume—Henry Kissinger and Jimmy Carter—became his friends and the repository of his confidence as he sought to enlist America in building a path toward peace with Israel and a new relationship between Egypt and the United States. He would have greatly admired a third contributor to this volume, James Baker, for his determined efforts to capitalize on another war—this time against Saddam Hussein—to bring the Arabs and Israelis to Madrid in October of 1991.

By first waging war, then making peace, Sadat made his own history. But he was indeed fortunate to have in Nixon, Ford, and Carter and in Kissinger and Vance American presidents and secretaries of state who understood the importance of Arab-Israeli peace to American interests, the value of cultivating Arab partners, and the need for tough and balanced diplomacy. Sadat also knew that American diplomacy was heavily oriented toward protecting Israel. But he banked successfully on the paradox of the partial mediator, in essence that he could use America's special relationship with Israel to get what he wanted, or at least, to paraphrase the Rolling Stones, to get what he needed. He probably knew all along that no Egyptian leader could redeem Palestine, but that he might redeem Egypt's honor, dignity, and land and maybe lay the basis for future progress. For this, he banked heavily on America not to deliver or impose a settlement but to use its power, credibility, and relationship with Israel to produce an equitable and durable peace.

A survey of the past decade of Arab-Israeli peacemaking would certainly have left Sadat's head spinning. Nowhere has the impact been greater than in the Palestinian arena where Arafat's death, failure to empower Mahmoud Abbas, Fatah's weakness, and Hamas's rise have put both the idea of a viable authoritative and pragmatic Palestinian center and a two-state solution at serious risk. It has indeed been a roller-coaster ride of highs and lows, bookended by two administrations—one Democratic and one Republican—with very different conceptions of America's role. As the administration of Barack Obama seeks to make Arab-Israeli peacemaking a top priority, it might be instructive to take a look at key ingredients for success. Some of these elements are reflected in the lectures contained in this volume. And it is quite appropriate that three of those lectures were delivered by the only three Americans—Carter, Kissinger, and Baker—who managed to succeed in Arab-Israeli peacemaking. It is worth looking to the past, not to be imprisoned by it, but to learn from it. History teaches many things, including prudence and perspective. Indeed, if you don't know where you've been, it's very hard to know where you're going.

Leadership

If Sadat had identified any single factor necessary to crack the frozen table of conflict and hatred born over generations, it would have been the capacity of strong leaders to act. The essays in this volume, focused as they are on Sadat, make that clear. No one would have appreciated or mourned more the death of strong leaders than Anwar Sadat. By 1999, the era of strong leadership in the Arab-Israeli arena was already drawing to a close. On the Israeli side, Yitzhak Rabin was dead, and Shimon Peres had been defeated again (this time by Netanyahu). His successor, Ehud Barak, proved to be bold and courageous in his peacemaking but also reckless, expecting to end conflict without offering what would be required and trying to do too much too quickly. By the late 1990s, when it came to peacemaking, Israel was a deeply divided society without a strong leader to pull it together. Indeed, with the failure of Camp David and the second intifada, the mood of the country was shifting rightward. When that strong prime minister came in the presence of Ariel Sharon, it was with a mandate to break the Palestinian intifada and position Israel well demographically and politically, not to do heroic peacemaking. But even here it took a strong and historically legitimate Israeli leader to unilaterally disengage from Gaza, dismantle settlements, and remove settlers. Sharon's successor—Ehud Olmert—would have liked to become a peacemaker, but because of his own imperfect options, found himself dragged into two wars instead in Lebanon and Gaza.

On the Arab side, things were not much better. By 2000, both Jordan's King Hussein and Syria's president Assad were dead. Their sons, Abdullah and Bashar, while providing continuity, seemed to lack the power, skill, and legitimacy of their fathers. Sitting on top of the Palestinian house, with the promise of Palestinian independence fading, was Yasir Arafat. He had, to be sure, missed an opportunity at Camp David not by his refusal to accept what Barak offered but in his unwillingness to negotiate in any meaningful sense of the word. Increasingly suspicious of Israel and America, he exploited the al-Aqsa intifada to improve his street credibility and

negotiating position and to remind the world he still had cards to play.

By the fall of 2000, Arafat was in survival mode. He would essentially remain in that role until his death in November 2004, a prisoner of a struggle that defined his political life. Arab-Israeli peacemaking is hard enough with powerful leaders; it is nearly impossible with those who are constrained and prisoners rather than masters of their political constituencies. Nor could Arafat's successor Mahmoud Abbas, a good man with even better intentions, master his own political house. By 2006, Hamas exploited Fatah's dysfunction and the misery of Palestinians under Israeli occupation and won in the Palestinian Legislative Council. A year later, Hamas had consolidated its control over Gaza.

Each of the lectures in this volume, though not intended as an analysis of leadership, essentially reaches the basic conclusion that nothing can happen without it. Without Sadat, as Kissinger and Carter attest, there would have been no Egyptian-Israeli peace treaty. Indeed by implication, Sadat also made Menachem Begin's response possible (heroic in its own way given the ideological distance that the Likud leader had to travel). This is as it must be. Given the existential risks and dangers that peacemaking poses to the political leader (Sadat and Rabin), diplomacy requires larger-than-life personalities to succeed.

Urgency

A second element related to leadership that is reflected in these lectures about Sadat is urgency.

Sadat was a man in a hurry. He saw the need for decisive action in war and in peace because he read his political map, Israel's, and America's correctly. And in his strategy, Sadat, as Kissinger made clear, created an opening that made the need for action on the part of Israel and the United States urgent as well. The logic of this approach is crucial to understanding why Arabs and Israelis make the decisions they do. Given how hard the issues are and the narrow margin for error, Arab and Israeli decision making becomes a set of calculations based on the severity of the pain and prospects of possible gain. If neither disincentives nor incentives are present in sufficient quantity, what results is the status quo no matter how unattractive it may appear to be to those of us who don't live in the neighborhood. And given the importance of getting mutual agreement, both pain and gain are necessary.

The pain-gain conceit explains all of the historic breakthroughs America helped orchestrate during the past fifty years. Sadat's war and peace strategy between 1973 and 1977 cracked the frozen table and enabled the United States first to negotiate Arab-Israeli disengagement agreements and then, courtesy of Sadat's November 1977 visit to Israel, to ultimately broker Egyptian-Israeli peace. The first Persian Gulf War shook the region enough to create an opening for a powerful America to bring Arabs and Israelis to the Madrid Peace Conference. And the first Palestinian intifada forced Rabin in the late 1980s and 1990s to begin to examine the possibility that only a political solution with the Palestinians would preserve Israel's character as a Jewish, democratic state. Oslo was the result. Indeed, it was that Israeli-Palestinian process, however flawed, that gave Jordan's King Hussein the cover to make peace with Israel.

The critical relevance of urgency today is that it's not just a matter of creating pain and discomfort. The status quo between Israelis and Palestinians is painful but not prohibitively so. And what's more, the incentives aren't evident, yet. The Gaza war—unlike the 1973 conflict, the first Persian Gulf War, or the first Palestinian intifada—had no silver linings. Whether one can be found or manufactured by the Obama administration together with the parties themselves may well hold the key to moving forward.

Harder Issues, Fair Resolution

Negotiating Egyptian-Israeli peace was tough. It was precedent setting. But with all due respect to Sadat, the issues in his negotiation with Menachem Begin paled in comparison to the degree of difficulty Arabs, Israelis, and Americans would tackle with their issues during the 1990s. In the 1970s, Sinai, normalization, and oil fields were hard. Jerusalem, borders, refugees have proven harder, much harder. These matters cut to the core of identity, religion, and historic trauma in a way the Egyptian-Israeli negotiating process did not. So too, Sadat's peace with Israel was quite separate, which, of course, made it manageable, especially for the Israelis. The prospect of moving on a comprehensive peace in which Israel (and its political system) has to manage withdrawal from the West Bank and Golan Heights, dismantle settlements and evacuate settlers on two fronts, and deal with Jerusalem together or even in close sequence is almost unimaginable. Still, it is critical to point out that regardless of the degree of difficulty, the Egyptian-Israeli peace treaty succeeded and has endured because it is based on a balance of interests. Whether it's a negotiation, a friendship, or a business deal, longevity depends on both sides getting what they need and getting it in a way they can defend before their political constituencies. Leaders need explanations before they do risky things to convince themselves; and part of that explanation is related to how easy it will be to defend what they have done in front of both their friends and adversaries. This logic applies both to democratic and more-authoritarian polities, particularly when the nation's honor and dignity is involved.

Arabs and Israelis alike will need peace agreements they can defend and that meet core needs and requirements. Nobody gets 100 percent. Even Sadat, who got 100 percent of Sinai, was forced to make fundamental adjustments to his broader strategy on a comprehensive framework that would include a Palestinian deal. He was strong enough to weather the changes of a separate peace in a way King Hussein, who used Oslo as cover, never could. Menachem Begin never planned to give up all of Sinai or dismantle settlements.

Still, while everyone must give, they must get enough to warrant the risks of giving. This balance of interests is critical. At Camp David, Ehud Barak put a bold set of ideas out that went further than any previous Israeli prime minister. But it wasn't nearly enough to meet Palestinian needs and requirements. Arafat's real transgression at the summit was not that he didn't accept what was being offered but that he didn't negotiate in any meaningful sense of the word. As George Mitchell's lecture suggests, a balance must be found that each side can accept.

It is no wonder, then, in the face of such challenges that the record of peacemaking during the past decade has been so poor. It has not been for lack of effort, at least during the final years of the Clinton administration when an American president with the best of intentions and tremendous commitment tried unsuccessfully to broker permanent status agreements between Israel, Syria, and the Palestinians. The lion's share for that failure rested with the locals, to be sure, but America did not help its own case by departing from its role as a tough, balanced mediator (Carter, Kissinger, and Baker) and becoming a more passive facilitator under Clinton. If failed diplomacy had negative consequences, the lack of interest and disengagement that has marked the administration of George W. Bush has been catastrophic. Looking back now, it is hard to believe that since Madrid in 1991, America has failed to broker one agreement of consequence between Arabs and Israelis that actually endured.

The Effective Mediator

The issue of balance brings us to the final element of the four essential ingredients necessary to have a chance to succeed at Arab-Israeli peacemaking. It's important to look briefly at the policies of both Bill Clinton and George W. Bush. In both cases, the United States failed to find the right role for itself. And although America isn't primarily responsible for the absence of Arab-Israeli peace, our actions and inactions are the single most important factors outside of the region that bear on the issue.

Bill Clinton inherited the best hand in Arab-Israeli peace process diplomacy of any American president. Within nine months of taking office, Israel and the Palestine Liberation Organization (PLO) had signed a ground-breaking declaration of principles, and Israeli prime minister Rabin had put the idea of full withdrawal from the Golan Heights in the secretary of state's pocket. Within a year, Israel and Jordan would lay the basis for a treaty of peace signed in October 1994. Yet, eight years later as Clinton left office, the entire negotiating process had collapsed in a paroxysm of terror and violence. What happened? What role did America play? And what would Sadat, had he lived, thought of the approach America had taken?

I have said before, but it is worth repeating, that Arabs and Israelis bear primary responsibility for this sad ending. This dysfunction flowed from the lack of clarity and honesty in the negotiations, something that Sadat would have decried. The contradictions in the Oslo process they negotiated, and Israeli, Syrian, and Palestinian unwillingness to understand what was required by each side to reach permanent-status agreements, let alone pay the necessary price, created flawed analysis, missed opportunities, and out-of-whack expectations that together doomed peace. Still, America was a central player during this period. It is fair to ask whether any mediator could have succeeded in overcoming these odds. But it is equally fair to posit that given America's operating style during those years, there was little chance of success and a fair bet we might even help make the situation worse.

Oslo's logic seemed sound on paper but not on the ground. From the beginning, Israelis and Palestinians had very different interpretations of the agreements and acted accordingly. For Arafat, Oslo was viewed as a device to gain recognition from Israel and America and to set the stage for either relatively quick independence or a return to struggle. For Israel, Oslo was a probation period to test Palestinian intentions by transferring land for assumption of security responsibilities and cooperation. Trust would accumulate gradually so that within a five-year transition period, Israelis and Palestinians could deal with the tougher issues of permanent status. One could only imagine how Sadat would have reacted to an interim process that never defined the end state or had a third party to assist Israelis and Palestinians in how to get there.

It never worked out that way. The Oslo years played out against the backdrop of the pernicious daily dynamic between the occupier and occupied without a third party to monitor or help them manage their problems. Israel continued to act unilaterally with closures, checkpoints, settlement activities, and land confiscation. Palestinians—both groups within the Palestinian Authority and those outside of it—exerting the power of the weak, resisted with violence and terror, even while at times moving to preempt and control it.

America didn't negotiate the Oslo accords, so it was not in the best position to influence them. But the Clinton administration really did not exert much of an effort. Having participated in these decisions directly, I can say we were never tough enough with the Israelis on settlement activity or with the Palestinians on violence or incitement in the media. During the 1996–99 period, we did get much more intensely involved in setting up monitoring mechanisms, but by then it was too late. As we prepared to go into an eleventh-hour push to broker an Israeli-Palestinian agreement at Camp David in July 2000, we never understood how negatively six years of broken promises and bad behaviors on the ground would color the resolve needed to deal with the big issues. We never tried hard enough to impose costs for these behaviors or to hold each side to its commitments. Oslo required a third party not to act as judge and jury but to work with both sides to monitor and help them resolve problems,

and, if necessary, to cajole and pressure. We forget that Sadat thought not in terms of direct negotiations with Israel but of an America acting as the full partner. One can only suspect that he would have warned the United States from the beginning that Oslo would never work without a strong American role. We were not there to play this role. And if we could not do it on the interim issues, how did we expect to be effective in brokering an agreement on the final status?

Having been unsuccessful in correcting or moderating the flaws of Oslo's interim process, the Clinton administration, driven by Barak's agenda and its own sense of urgency, acquiesced in the prime minister's bid to do the impossible: conclude agreements with Syria and the Palestinians by the end of the president's term. It was not the focus on the big issues that was the problem. The interim approach had played itself out, a serious Israeli-Palestinian confrontation was looming, the parties needed a vision of where Oslo was headed, and the Clinton administration was coming to an end. What got America into trouble was its willingness to enable a make-or-break Israeli approach and our lack of understanding of what it would take to reach conflict-ending agreements and of the resolve to help broker them.

Instead of critically evaluating Barak's strategy—Syria first, while putting Palestinians on hold—we enabled it without sufficient regard to whether or not it made sense for our interests or for the overall interests of the negotiations. Between the fall of 1999 and the spring of 2000, we let Israel define the agenda, did not know how to close an Israeli-Syrian deal, and were not honest with ourselves or Barak about what it would take to do so. Assad was not going to settle for less than the June 4, 1967, line, however elusive and hard it was to define. Nor were we clear or honest enough with Syria. If Assad wanted 100 percent of the Golan, he would have to help craft a peacemaking process that went well beyond his niggardly view of what peace entailed. He would have to reach out to the Israelis in secret as well as use public diplomacy. One wonders how Sadat would have counseled American negotiators as they faced the tension between the Syrian and Palestinian tracks. Sadat, although understanding the importance of comprehensive settlement, was always wary of Assad's motives. Would he have advised the Syrian president to try secret contacts with Israel as he had done?

By July 2000, having failed to produce an Israeli-Syrian agreement, Barak now pushed for an all-or-nothing summit with Arafat for which neither was adequately prepared. Neither were we. Ending conflict (Barak's goal) would have required moves on borders, refugees, and Jerusalem that went beyond anyone's capacity to consider in the summer of 2000. It would have also mandated a strong American role at the summit, including putting out and sticking by our own proposals. The summit's failure combined with our decision (again

pushed by Barak) to blame Arafat—and the Palestinian leader's willingness to ride the violence that broke out in September—all but guaranteed deterioration. However well intentioned the president's decision was to lay out his parameters on final status that December, it was too little, too late. These ideas might well provide the basis for serious negotiations one day, but not in the fall of 2000. Clinton left office (Barak was to follow in February 2001) against the backdrop of a severe and bloody Israeli-Palestinian confrontation.

If the Clinton administration was really determined to reach agreements, it should have calculated more accurately what it would take to close and what Barak, Arafat, and Assad required. It seems fantastical on reflection to believe that agreements on both fronts could have been reached within a year, given the choices confronting Arabs and Israelis. After all, they had only been dealing seriously with permanent status—at least on the Israeli-Palestinian track for barely a year. These issues raised tremendous political, psychological, and even existential challenges for both sides. There was no way they could be resolved quickly or easily.

Part of our problem was using Israeli requirements to determine our own and to guide the negotiating process. We tended to dismiss Assad's stated need for 100 percent of the Golan and Arafat's need for a settlement very close to the June 4, 1967, lines as a negotiating tactic while accepting Barak's unwillingness to give more as a true bottom-line position. The fact is the only precedent we had for a final deal between Israel and the Arabs was the Egyptian-Israeli peace treaty. Here, Sadat got 100 percent of Sinai, plus the dismantling of all settlements there. Had Sadat been around in 2000, he would have been an invaluable source and repository of advice on more accurately reading both the Syrians and the Palestinians. Indeed, America could have used him for the reality therapy that was lacking during this entire period.

Instead of trying to talk the Arabs out of their needs, we should have made clear what price they would have to pay to achieve them. This would have required a much more honest and forceful conversation with both sides about bottom lines. Had we been able to do this, we would have known how big the gaps were and whether and how they could be closed. In eight years of on-again, off-again Israeli-Syrian negotiations, we were never on the verge of closing. Worse still, in the year 2000 we hosted three presidential meetings—at Shepherdstown, Geneva, and Camp David. They all failed, and failure only reinforced American weakness as an effective mediator.

Failure would also do something else: convince the new administration that serious American efforts on Arab-Israeli peace could not possibly succeed. If Bill Clinton was too passive a facilitator, George W. Bush disengaged from serious efforts. The origin of that disengagement lay in three factors that by the end of the administration's first year had effectively taken America out of the peace business.

First, the new administration inherited a terrible set of circumstances: a new, tough-minded Israeli prime minister whose mandate was breaking the second intifada; a besieged and combative Yasir Arafat determined to struggle on; and an ongoing Israeli-Palestinian war marked by suicide terror inside Israel. Neither side was interested in a cease-fire or an interim agreement. And the Bush administration had no intention of putting itself in the middle of a crisis that it did not know how to resolve.

Second, the violence only reinforced the administration's instincts to stay away. The new president came into office determined to change the face of America's foreign policy, at least as presented by his predecessor. It was the ABC phenomenon (anybody or anything but Clinton). The former president's high-wire diplomacy at Camp David had never been very compelling to the president or his inner circle, who never considered the Arab-Israeli issue a priority in protecting America's interests in the Middle East anyway. Besides, diplomacy might mean dealing with Arafat and maybe even tension with Israel, neither of which was very appealing to a new team already increasingly focused on Iraq.

Finally, in the wake of 9/11, the Arab-Israeli issue vanished as a priority. The focus now was fighting terror and addressing the root causes of the region's lack of stability and peace—rogue states and authoritarian regimes. Democratic Israel was increasingly seen as a vital ally in a sea of dictators.

September 11 would paradoxically generate a burst of peace-process activity to placate and attract allies in the looming war against terror. That fall, in speeches by the president and secretary of state, America laid out its support for a Palestinian state. The administration would even appoint a special envoy, retired U.S. Central Command chief Anthony Zinni, to broker an Israeli-Palestinian cease-fire. But these efforts were more of a box-checking exercise than an attempt at serious diplomacy.

By the spring of 2002—with violence increasing and Arafat seen as its root cause—the president gave a speech on June 24 essentially endorsing a Palestinian state if the Palestinians instituted reforms and changed their leadership. The speech made clear that the logic of Arab-Israeli peace was no longer just about negotiating grievances and differences; now it involved more transformative matters. The Arab-Israeli conflict had become a battle between democrats and dictators, moderates and extremists, and terrorists and counterterrorists. Israel was not perfect, as its settlement policies demonstrated, but in the war against terror, it was seen to be an ally. Arafat and his cronies, let alone Hamas and Islamic jihad, were not.

The June 24 speech would park and reframe the Arab-Israeli issue. A year later, in June 2003, President Bush met with Prime Minister Sharon and the new Palestinian prime minister Mahmoud Abbas in Jordan. In the wake of what appeared to be a successful American effort in Iraq, the meeting was ostensibly designed to discuss how to implement the newly minted Quartet road map to peace. But continuing violence, Sharon's and Arafat's unwillingness to agree to a security-and-political approach to stop it, and the administration's reluctance to get involved guaranteed no movement. Within a year, Sharon was planning how Israel could disengage unilaterally from Gaza. That disengagement took place during September 2005 with the administration's full support. If diplomacy couldn't produce Israeli withdrawal and dismantling of settlements, maybe unilateral moves could. The consequences of this approach, with its lack of Palestinian reciprocity and Israeli-Palestinian coordination, would soon become painfully clear.

Still, Arafat's death in November 2004 and the election of Abbas as president in January 2005 created a unique opportunity to capitalize on a new Palestinian leadership, which is what the administration had wanted all along. Instead of moving quickly to empower Abbas and to push for Israeli-Palestinian negotiations, even on interim issues, the Bush administration hesitated. A year later in January 2006, Hamas won a majority in the Palestinian Legislative Council. Within two years it was cohabiting with Abbas in a national unity government engineered by the Saudis. Palestinian unity was short-lived. A divided, dysfunctional Fatah was no match for a more organized, determined Hamas. In June 2007, Hamas preempted efforts to strengthen Abbas in Gaza by seizing its military positions and handing it a resounding defeat on the streets. The new secretary of state, who had since the fall of 2006, taken a more active interest in trying to promote Israeli-Palestinian negotiations, now faced a situation that made any progress on a political horizon difficult to envision. Neither the Annapolis conference in the fall of 2007 nor the hours of negotiation between Abbas and Olmert throughout 2008 made much of an impact. By the time of Barack Obama's inauguration, the Bush administration watched most of the legacy on Arab-Israeli peacemaking get buried in the violence of the 2008–09 Israeli-Hamas confrontation in Gaza.

The last ten years of America's involvement in Arab-Israeli issues reads like a story of missed opportunities and of those never explored and an ever-deteriorating situation on the ground. Whether the United States can regain its footing in Arab-Israeli diplomacy will depend to a large extent on local factors beyond its control. In a sense, the region has changed too much, and the administration has sat on the sidelines too long to expect quick or easy turnarounds. A combination of weak and constrained leaders on the Arab and Israeli side, powerful non-state actors (Hamas and Hizbollah) backed by Syria and Iran, and the American failure in Iraq have created a regional environment not terribly hospitable for bold decisions in peacemaking.

Both the viability of an authoritative, pragmatic Palestinian center and a two-state solution are now increasingly at risk. And the lessons of disengagement are painfully clear. America cannot create serious negotiations, but without its attention and focus during periods of crisis and opportunity, not much of lasting value can emerge. Never say never in terms of hopes for Arab-Israeli peacemaking. But the Obama administration should not push its luck. In a post-9/11 world, managing and resolving the Arab-Israeli conflict, no matter how difficult, must be a vital American interest. Anwar Sadat would have been the first to admit that American security, and that of its Arab and Israeli friends in the region, depends on it. And he would have pushed the Bush administration to do more during its first four years and to be smarter during its second four to move the Arab-Israeli issue forward.

But Sadat would also be the first to concede that the key to starting, if not sustaining, any serious peacemaking effort is leadership and the political will and courage that go along with it. In existential conflicts like the Arab-Israeli clash—which are driven by memory, identity, and religion—home-grown leadership is indispensable. And for the past decade or so, it has been missing in sufficient quantities on both the Arab and Israeli sides.

Leadership of Sadat's magnitude and quality is almost impossible to replicate. As the essays in this book attest, his contribution was idiosyncratic. After Sadat, the mold was broken. As the lectures raised in tribute to him in this volume show, the need to look fairly and honestly at what both sides need to make a peace agreement, the imperative of a major American role, and the urgent need for a solution are critically important for the future. With these factors and strong leadership from both sides, there is a chance for meaningful Arab-Israeli peace. And that would be the most fitting tribute of all to Anwar Sadat's memory and legacy.

CONTRIBUTORS

Shibley Telhami is the Anwar Sadat Professor for Peace and Development at the University of Maryland, College Park, and a nonresident senior fellow at the Saban Center at the Brookings Institution. He received his doctorate in political science from the University of California at Berkeley. He has served as adviser to the U.S. Mission to the UN (1990–91), as adviser to former Congressman Lee Hamilton, and as a member of the U.S. delegation to the Trilateral U.S.-Israeli-Palestinian Anti-Incitement Committee. He also served on the Iraq Study Group as a member of the Strategic Environment Working Group. Among numerous publications is his best-selling book, *The Stakes: America and the Middle East*. He is a member of the Council on Foreign Relations and serves on the board of the Education for Employment Foundation as well as several academic boards. He has also served on the boards of the United States Institute of Peace and Human Rights Watch. Professor Telhami received the 2002 University of Maryland Distinguished International Service Award and the 2006 University System of Maryland Board of Regents Excellence in Public Service Award.

Aaron David Miller is a public policy scholar at the Woodrow Wilson International Center for scholars in Washington, D.C. He has advised Republican and Democratic secretaries of state on Arab-Israeli negotiations. He recently authored *The Much Too Promised Land: America's Elusive Search for Arab-Israeli Peace,* and his new book *Can America Have Another Great President?* will be published in 2012.

Dr. Jehan Sadat was the first lady of Egypt from 1970 to 1981. She earned a master's degree and a PhD from Cairo University. One of her first projects was Talla Society, a cooperative designed to bring personal, social, and economic empowerment of illiterate, impoverished Egyptian village women. She founded Egypt's Wafa' Wal Amal, the first and largest rehabilitation center in the Middle East. She also founded the Arab-African Women's League. She is the author of several books, including her best-selling autobiography, *A Woman of Egypt*, and *My Hope for Peace*, published in 2009. Currently a fellow at the Center for International Development and Conflict Management at the University of Maryland, College Park, Dr. Sadat is a recipient of many international awards for public service and humanitarian efforts for women and children and of more than twenty honorary doctorate degrees from national and international colleges and universities.

UNITED STATES INSTITUTE OF PEACE PRESS

Since its inception, the United States Institute of Peace Press has published over 150 books on the prevention, management, and peaceful resolution of international conflicts—among them such venerable titles as Raymond Cohen's *Negotiating Across Cultures*; *Herding Cats* and *Leashing the Dogs of War* by Chester A. Crocker, Fen Osler Hampson, and Pamela Aall; and I. William Zartman's *Peacemaking and International Conflict*. All our books arise from research and fieldwork sponsored by the Institute's many programs. In keeping with the best traditions of scholarly publishing, each volume undergoes both thorough internal review and blind peer review by external subject experts to ensure that the research, scholarship, and conclusions are balanced, relevant, and sound. As the Institute prepares to move to its new headquarters on the National Mall in Washington, D.C., the Press is committed to extending the reach of the Institute's work by continuing to publish significant and sustainable works for practitioners, scholars, diplomats, and students.

—*Valerie Norville, Director*

ABOUT THE UNITED STATES INSTITUTE OF PEACE

The United States Institute of Peace is an independent, nonpartisan institution established and funded by Congress. The Institute provides analysis, training, and tools to help prevent, manage, and end violent international conflicts, promote stability, and professionalize the field of peacebuilding.

Chairman of the Board: J. Robinson West
Vice Chairman: George E. Moose
President: Richard H. Solomon
Executive Vice President: Tara Sonenshine
Chief Financial Officer: Michael Graham

BOARD OF DIRECTORS

J. Robinson West (Chair), Chairman, PFC Energy, Washington, D.C.
George E. Moose (Vice Chairman), Adjunct Professor of Practice, The George Washington University
Anne H. Cahn, Former Scholar in Residence, American University
Chester A. Crocker, James R. Schlesinger Professor of Strategic Studies, School of Foreign Service, Georgetown University
Ikram U. Khan, President, Quality Care Consultants, LLC
Kerry Kennedy, Human Rights Activist
Stephen D. Krasner, Graham H. Stuart Professor of International Relations, Stanford University
Jeremy A. Rabkin, Professor, George Mason School of Law
Judy Van Rest, Executive Vice President, International Republican Institute
Nancy Zirkin, Executive Vice President, Leadership Conference on Civil Rights

Members ex officio
Michael H. Posner, Assistant Secretary of State for Democracy, Human Rights, and Labor
James N. Miller, Principal Deputy Under Secretary of Defense for Policy
Ann E. Rondeau, Vice Admiral, U.S. Navy, President, National Defense University
Richard H. Solomon, President, United States Institute of Peace (nonvoting)

The Sadat Lectures

Text: Adobe Garamond
Display Text: Univers 45 Light
Cover Design: Katie Sweetman, New York, NY
Interior Design: Katie Sweetman, New York, NY
Page Makeup: Christian Feuerstein